Insider's Guide to

K–12 EDUCATION IN BC

What every parent and educator needs to know

Published by Pacific Educational Press
The University of British Columbia

Publisher: Susan Howell
Managing Editor: Katrina Petrik
Developmental Editors: Katrina Petrik, Elizabeth Salomons
Production Manager: Elizabeth Salomons
Designers: Celia Bell, Sharlene Eugenio
Copy Editor: Nancy Wilson
Proofreader: Grace Yaginuma

Cover Image: Sutherland Secondary School, North Vancouver,
British Columbia
Cover Photographer: Celia Bell

18 17 16 15   1 2 3 4

ABOUT THE AUTHORS

David Mushens is a vice-principal at École Cariboo Hill Secondary School in School District No. 41 (Burnaby). He has presented workshops to educators and parents on topics such as teaching standards, assessment and evaluation, educational leadership, labour relations, and poverty's impact on learners. With co-author Faizel Rawji, he has presented workshops on school leadership to Aga Khan Education Services' headmasters in Kenya.

David has published two novels, written commentary for numerous media outlets, and presented a paper to the national conference of the Canadian Association for the Practical Study of Law in Education.

Faizel Rawji is the principal at Sunnyside Elementary School in School District No. 36 (Surrey). He has served as an advisor for the Premier's Technology Council and contributed to the BC Education Plan in areas ranging from technology education to healthy living standards. A recipient of Canada's Outstanding Principals Award and the Surrey Now Community Leader Award, he serves as the president of the Surrey Principals' and Vice-Principals' Association.

In addition to his work with co-author David Mushens in Kenya, Faizel has been appointed to the Aga Khan's national education board, providing strategy and advice for the Ismaili community.

David Starr is the principal of Byrne Creek Community School in School District No. 41 (Burnaby). David has authored a book, *From Bombs to Books*, that shares the deeply moving stories of refugee students, their parents, and the staff at Edmonds and Byrne Creek Community Schools. He has also written a novel for young adults that will be published in 2016.

David has spoken nationally and internationally on issues around community and refugee education. His schools have been featured by numerous media outlets. He is a Vancouver Canuck Community MVP Award winner and a member of the board of directors of Canada Scores Vancouver, a charity dedicated to providing literacy, soccer, and leadership opportunities to inner city youth.

CONTENTS

LIST OF ABBREVIATIONS

ACEbc	Association for Community Education in British Columbia
ACE IT	Accelerated Credit Enrollment in Industry Training
AIP	Annual Instructional Plan
AP	Advanced Placement program
BCASBO	BC Association of School Business Officials
BCCPAC	BC Confederation of Parent Advisory Councils
BCPSEA	BC Public School Employers' Association
BCPVPA	BC Principals' and Vice-Principals' Association
BCSSA	BC School Superintendents Association
BCSTA	BC School Trustees Association
BCTF	BC Teachers' Federation
CSF	Conseil scolaire francophone de la Colombie-Britannique
CUPE	Canadian Union of Public Employees
DPA	Daily Physical Activity requirement
DPAC	District Parent Advisory Council
EA	Education Assistant
ELL	English Language Learner
ESL	English as a Second Language (now referred to as ELL)
FSA	Foundation Skills Assessment
IB	International Baccalaureate program
IDS	Independent Directed Studies
IEP	Individual Education Plan
IRP	Integrated Resource Package
ITA	Industry Training Authority
MACC	Multi-Age Cluster Class
PAC	Parent Advisory Council
PLO	Prescribed Learning Outcome
SLP	Speech–Language Pathologist
SSA	Secondary School Apprenticeship
TOC	Teacher on Call
TRB	Teacher Regulation Branch of the BC Ministry of Education

INSIDE THIS BOOK

The following features will help you navigate the information in *Insider's Guide to K–12 Education in BC*.

PART 3

Program and Schooling Options

KEY QUESTIONS

- What program and schooling options are avail[...] child?
- What are the benefits of each option?
- Is one of these options the rig[...]

Key Questions

Each part opens with questions addressed in the following pages to help you quickly find the information you need.

margins

balanced-calendar school: a school that operates on a year-round calendar, with classes typically in session for three months, followed by a one-month break

[...] that may earn the[...]

[...]al Instructional Plan (AIP): a lear[...]
[...]arner

assessment: an ongoing process that helps [...] how well students are learning; is not grade[...]

balanced-calendar school: a school that operates [...] with classes typically in session for three months, fol[...]

BC Certificate of Graduation (Dogwood Diploma): [...] of Education upon completion of the Graduation Prog[...]

BC Teachers' Federation (BCTF): the union represe[...] teachers in British Columbia

board of education: a board of school trustees th[...] schools; usually called a school board

[...]tchment area: the area defined by the sc[...] [...]ular school

[...]ram: a program [...]

back of book

Glossary Terms

Key terms related to K–12 education are defined in the margins and at the back of the book on pages 124–126.

9

Links

The magnifying glass icon indicates that further information about the topic may be found in online resources listed at the back of the book on pages 127–133.

margins

back of book

Employee Group

Due to recent hig
Columbians that th
That said, labour
all that common
days lost to str
illness, e

@

PART 1 How the School Syst

GOVERNANCE AND ADMINISTRATION

Ministry of Education

BC Ministry of Education: http://www.gov.bc.ca/bced/

BC Ministry of Education *Manual of School Law* (includes links
   Teachers Act, Independent School Act, and *First Nations Edu*
   www2.gov.bc.ca/gov/content/education-training/administ
   policy/manual-of-school-law

BC Ministry of Education—Teacher Regulation Branch:
   https://www.bcteacherregulation.ca/

Board of Education

BC Ministry of Education—Directory of BC K–12 School an
   Information: http://www.bced.gov.bc.ca/apps/imcl/i

BC Ministry of Education—Discover Your School:
   http://www.discoveryourschool.gov.bc.ca

chool

rs' Federation (BCTF): htt

INTRODUCTION

School administrators get a *lot* of questions about how things work in the school system, for example: *How do I choose the right school for my child? There are so many options available, from French immersion to International Baccalaureate; how do I choose the right one for my child? What happens if my child needs extra support at school?* and *How is my child's learning assessed?*

Like any field, education has its own jargon, procedures, and practices. Those of us immersed in it sometimes forget that schools and schooling can be complicated, and that the way we do business can be mystifying, confusing, and unclear—until now.

Insider's Guide to K–12 Education in BC is your guide to understanding the structures, choices, and issues you're likely to encounter in the school system. You will learn how the school system works and discover educational choices you may not have known about. With this knowledge, you will be in a position of strength to advocate for and support your children as they navigate through the school system.

This book is organized into six parts.

Part 1: How the School System Works

The first section outlines how the overall school system works: how schools and districts are run and funded; how schools are organized; and what curriculum students are taught.

Part 2: Choosing a School

Part 2 explains what makes a good school *good*, and what you should consider when choosing a public or independent school for your child. It also outlines the steps for enrolling a child in your chosen school.

Part 3: Program and Schooling Options

This section provides you with information about the wide variety of schools and programs of choice that exist in both the public and independent schools of British Columbia. It can help you decide what programs would be a good fit for your child.

Part 4: Learning Support and Behaviour Interventions

Part 4 explains the important topics of special needs, learning assistance, English language learning, bullying, and behaviour interventions.

Part 5: Assessment and Evaluation

This section explains how teachers assess and evaluate student learning. It provides an overview of report cards, performance standards and letter grades, the Foundation Skills Assessment (FSA) tests, and provincial exams.

Part 6: Frequently Asked Questions

The final section of the book answers a variety of questions about schooling, including: *What input can I have in my child's class placement? What happens on professional development days?* and *How can I support my child's learning at home?*

Insider's Guide to K–12 Education in BC answers your questions before you even ask them. Parents will find the information they need to make the best decisions for their children, at any stage of their Kindergarten to Grade 12 education. Educators will find the information they need to help parents navigate the school system. This book is not about educational theory: it's a practical guide, with real-life answers to real-life situations.

School's in! It's time to get to work!

PART 1

How the School System Works

KEY QUESTIONS

- How is the school system governed? What are the roles and responsibilities of the Ministry of Education, school districts, and schools?

- How is the school system funded?

- How are grade levels organized in the Kindergarten to Grade 12 (K–12) system?

- How is the school year organized?

- Who determines what students are taught?

GOVERNANCE AND ADMINISTRATION

In Canada, education is governed at the provincial level. Like most public and private organizations, the British Columbia school system is based on a hierarchy:

- At the top is the Ministry of Education, led by the Minister of Education and senior ministry officials.
- Below the Ministry of Education are the school district boards of education (often called *school boards*), composed of locally elected school trustees. Boards of education appoint superintendents to oversee the programs and operations of the school district.
- Schools operate under the direction of the school boards and are usually led by a principal, with input from a Parent Advisory Council (PAC).

There are variations to the governance structures within school districts and schools. The following pages describe the laws, regulations, and policies under which all of British Columbia's public schools must operate.

Ministry of Education

The BC Ministry of Education serves two functions: political and professional-educational.

The structure of British Columbia's public school system

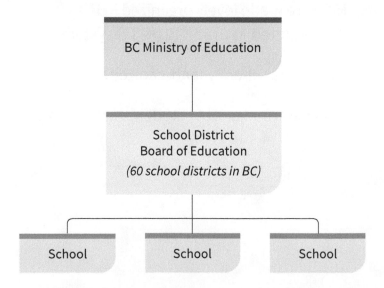

Political Functions

The **Ministry of Education** is headed by the Minister of Education, who is a member of the cabinet of the government of British Columbia and an elected member of the legislative assembly. He or she is responsible for

- ensuring that the government's education platform is implemented
- managing, updating, and revising legislation that governs schools throughout the province
- aligning political promises and ideology with the law outlined in British Columbia's *Manual of School Law*

Ministry of Education: the body designated by the provincial government to oversee K–12 education

The *Manual of School Law* includes the following pieces of legislation:

- *School Act*: the rules by which the entire system is run
- *Teachers Act*: the rules concerning teacher certification and regulation
- *Independent School Act*: the rules that govern how independent schools work
- *First Nations Education Act*: the rules that recognize the rights of First Nations peoples over education in their traditional territories

Professional-Educational Functions

The Ministry of Education's professional-educational staff work under the direction of the Minister of Education, and are responsible for the overall administration of education throughout British Columbia. The most senior unelected ministry official is the Deputy Minister of Education, who leads the ministry staff. Among other duties, the staff are responsible for

- required curriculum and program delivery
- required examinations and marking
- graduation from secondary school and certification
- assessment and evaluation of student learning
- information technology in school programs
- management of student and school data
- teacher qualification and certification (administered through the **Teacher Regulation Branch** of the Ministry of Education)
- strategic projects, such as improving environmental footprints and career program initiatives

Teacher Regulation Branch (TRB): the body of the Ministry of Education that governs teacher certification and discipline

Board of Education

Public schools across the province are organized into school districts, usually grouped by city or region. Districts are directed by boards of education (school boards) made up of school trustees. School trustees are, by law, elected to a four-year term during municipal elections. There are currently 60 school districts in British Columbia.

Depending on the school district, a trustee may represent a civic political party or a particular region of a rural school district that is geographically large. For example, school trustees in School District No. 39 (Vancouver) represent political parties, while School District No. 78 (Fraser-Cascade) has trustee representation from the communities of Agassiz, Hope, Harrison Hot Springs, and Boston Bar, guaranteeing each town in the district representation on the board.

school district: a geographical area, as defined by the *School Act*

board of education: a board of school trustees that oversees the district's public schools; usually called a *school board*

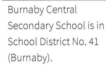

Burnaby Central Secondary School is in School District No. 41 (Burnaby).

Responsibilities

The school board scts the overall direction of the school district, including any local initiatives or policies. Decisions are made by vote. The structure of a school district mirrors the political/professional-educational model of the Ministry of Education. Trustees are the political wing and control governance and policy. Day-to-day operations of the school district are delegated to the **superintendent** and other district staff, including secretary-treasurers and assistant superintendents.

The authority of a school board is limited by a number of factors:

superintendent: the chief administrator of a school district, as designated by the school board

- **Budget**
  The school board determines how to spend the money it receives from the provincial government, but with most of the funding dedicated to salaries and staff benefits, there is little discretionary spending. To generate additional funds, many school boards recruit tuition-paying international students.

- **Curriculum**
  School boards may authorize locally developed courses in subject areas that are not covered in the Ministry of Education curriculum. These courses may count toward elective course credits for graduation. (See page 35 for more information about graduation requirements.)

- **Policies**
  School boards may enact policies specific to their district, but they must not conflict with provincial laws or regulations such as the *School Act*, or with rights guaranteed by the *Canadian Charter of Rights and Freedoms*.

- **Directives from the BC Ministry of Education**
  At the time of publication of this book, the government has introduced Bill 11: *Education Statutes Amendment Act*, which is expected to pass into law. The Act specifies that the minister may issue directives to school boards, which may include implementing special programs and projects or using a designated supplier of materials or equipment.

British Columbia School Districts

Note: School District No. 93 (Conseil scolaire francophone) is not confined to a geographical area of the province because it includes all francophone public schools in British Columbia.

5 Southeast Kootenay	50 Haida Gwaii	74 Gold Trail
6 Rocky Mountain	51 Boundary	78 Fraser-Cascade
8 Kootenay Lake	52 Prince Rupert	81 Fort Nelson
10 Arrow Lakes	53 Okanagan Similkameen	82 Coast Mountains
19 Revelstoke	54 Bulkley Valley	83 North Okanagan-Shuswap
20 Kootenay-Columbia	57 Prince George	84 Vancouver Island West
22 Vernon	58 Nicola-Similkameen	85 Vancouver Island North
23 Central Okanagan	59 Peace River South	87 Stikine
27 Cariboo-Chilcotin	60 Peace River North	91 Nechako Lakes
28 Quesnel	67 Okanagan Skaha	92 Nisga'a
47 Powell River	72 Campbell River	
48 Sea to Sky	73 Kamloops/Thompson	
49 Central Coast		

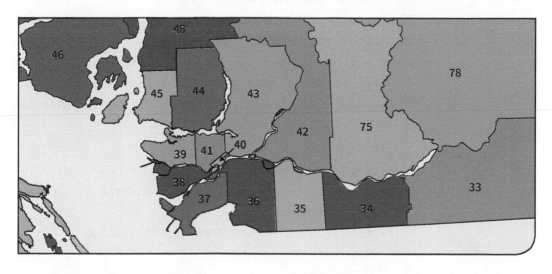

Lower Mainland inset

33 *Chilliwack*
34 *Abbotsford*
35 *Langley*
36 *Surrey*
37 *Delta*
38 *Richmond*

39 *Vancouver*
40 *New Westminster*
41 *Burnaby*
42 *Maple Ridge–Pitt Meadows*
43 *Coquitlam*

44 *North Vancouver*
45 *West Vancouver*
46 *Sunshine Coast*
48 *Sea to Sky*
75 *Mission*
78 *Fraser-Cascade*

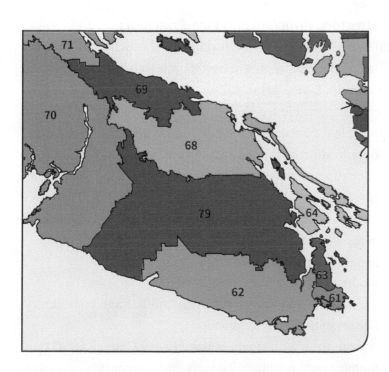

Southern Vancouver Island inset

61 *Greater Victoria*
62 *Sooke*
63 *Saanich*

64 *Gulf Islands*
68 *Nanaimo-Ladysmith*
69 *Qualicum*

70 *Alberni*
71 *Comox Valley*
79 *Cowichan Valley*

School Board Staff Responsibilities

The school district's operations are delegated to the superintendent and other district staff by the school board. School board staff work under the direction of the superintendent. Their responsibilities include supervision of school-based staff, management of the district and its resources, and implementation of policies and programs.

The responsibilities of district staff include

- resolution of concerns not settled at the school level (and if resolution cannot be found, the issue may be appealed to the school board)
- maintenance of all facilities within the district
- human resources management
- financial management of all district resources, including budgeting and accounting

School

The vast majority of decisions governing the day-to-day operation of the school are, in fact, made at the school itself.

Administrators: Principal and Vice-Principals

Within the school, authority rests with the principal or delegate. Under the *School Act*, every public school must have at least a principal, vice-principal, or director of instruction who is directly responsible for the school. The principal or delegate is responsible for a variety of school-based decisions, including

- organization of classes, classrooms, and teaching areas
- allocation of resources (including books, supplies, furniture, and so on) given to the school from the district office
- health and safety of students, teachers, and other personnel
- repairs and maintenance of the facility and equipment
- supervision of teachers and support staff
- student behaviour and deportment
- communication and liaison with families and community
- liaison with support agencies
- consultation with the Parent Advisory Council (PAC)
- management of school budgets and expenses
- compliance with directives and policies of the Ministry of Education and school board

Teachers

Ultimately, most educational and learning decisions are made directly by classroom teachers, the professionals who work most closely with students. Teachers generally have the autonomy to make a variety of decisions, including

- planning and implementation of individual lessons and units of study
- methods of instruction
- selection of instructional resources
- methods of assessment and evaluation
- management of student behaviour

Teachers must cover the required learning outcomes and comply with regulations of the *School Act* and other provincial laws, as well as any policies enacted by the local school board.

Effective teachers instill in their students a love of learning and challenge them to achieve their best.

BC Teachers'
Federation
(BCTF): the union
representing all
public school
teachers in British
Columbia

collective
agreement: a
legally binding
agreement between
an employer
and a group of
its unionized
employees

Employee Groups

Due to recent high profile strikes, it is well known to British Columbians that the public school system is a unionized workplace. That said, labour disruptions to BC's public school system are not all that common. Since 1995, there have been fewer than 50 school days lost to strikes, which is fewer than most students miss due to illness, extracurricular activities, and family vacations.

All public school teachers in British Columbia must belong to the **BC Teachers' Federation (BCTF)**. Since 1995, teachers have bargained collectively with the province through the BCTF. That is, while there are local provisions in **collective agreements** that apply only to an individual school district and its local teachers' association, the major items in the agreement, such as wages and benefits, are bargained at the provincial level for all 40 000 teachers in British Columbia.

In most of British Columbia's school districts, support staff such as office clerks, custodians, education assistants, maintenance personnel, and bus drivers are also unionized. Most are represented by the Canadian Union of Public Employees (CUPE).

Principals and vice-principals, directors of instruction, superintendents, and secretary-treasurers are not part of the BCTF bargaining unit. That is why school administrators report to work whenever teachers or support workers are on strike. Most management staff belong to professional associations, such as the

- BC Principals' and Vice-Principals' Association (BCPVPA)
- BC School Superintendents Association (BCSSA)
- BC Association of School Business Officials (BCASBO)

Elected school trustees may belong to the BC School Trustees Association (BCSTA). The BCSTA supports trustees in their work to improve student learning and assists its members with professional development, advocacy, and communications with government and other educational stakeholders.

School boards must belong to the BC Public School Employers' Association (BCPSEA), which is the accredited bargaining agent for all public school boards.

Parents and Guardians

While parents do not hold a formal role in the governance structure of the school system, they do have both formal and informal *advisory* roles that contribute to the decision-making process.

The **Parent Advisory Council (PAC)** is elected from within the parent community to advise the school leadership about issues of concern, plans for school growth and development, initiatives, school events, and even the structure of the school day and the calendar of the school year. PACs receive yearly provincial grants, which they use to purchase items that enhance and supplement the school experience.

Many school Parent Advisory Councils belong to a **District Parent Advisory Council (DPAC)**, with representatives from all schools in the district. DPACs come together to share information and provide input on matters involving many or all of the district's schools, such as the school district budget, the opening or closing of a school in the district, and district-wide programs.

The BC Confederation of Parent Advisory Councils (BCCPAC) provides input on matters affecting schools and learners throughout the province.

At the time of publication of this book, schools also have School Planning Councils. However, the government has introduced Bill 11: *Education Statutes Amendment Act*, which is expected to be passed in the legislative assembly. Once passed, this Act will eliminate School Planning Councils from the school governance structure.

Parent Advisory Council (PAC): an advisory board made up of parents of students registered in a school

District Parent Advisory Council (DPAC): an advisory board at the district level, made up of representatives of PACs from all schools in the district

FINANCE

The BC government budgeted $4.725 billion for K–12 education for the 2014/2015 school year.[1] Money is allocated to each district based on the number of students enrolled, established by a formal count done each school year at the end of September. In 2014/2015, school districts received $6900 per student enrolled in standard educational programs.[2]

In addition to the operating grant, funds are provided to school districts in order to address

- unique student needs (for example, those of English Language Learners, students with special educational requirements, Aboriginal students, and adult learners)
- declining enrollment (that is, when reduced funding based on fewer students would cause significant hardship)
- salary differentials for districts with higher-than-average teacher salaries (for example, when there are more experienced teachers who are at the maximum salary scale)
- unique geographical features (such as districts with significant transportation or heating costs)
- the Education Fund (a provision of the recent collective agreement with teachers, designed to provide a greater number of teachers to support class size and class composition issues)
- funding protection (that is, to protect highly valued programs that may otherwise be cancelled due to lower enrollment or high cost)

class composition: the number of students with special needs in a classroom

Where Does the Money Go?

The school district budget is used to pay for

- salaries and benefits of teachers, support staff, administrators, and other professionals (including education assistants, school psychologists, speech pathologists, specialists to help students with hearing and vision impairment, occupational therapists, and behavioural specialists)
- Teachers on Call and other substitute staff
- supplies and services
- repairs and capital upgrades to schools
- student transportation costs
- utilities
- insurance
- legal fees
- lease and rental costs

Teacher on Call (TOC): a teacher who replaces the permanent teacher during a temporary absence (for example, due to illness); also called a substitute teacher

School district budgets have little room for adjustment. Increases in costs such as supplies, hydro, and gas are not funded by the province, nor are some increased labour costs such as Employment Insurance premiums for employees. Salaries are by far the largest cost to districts and, in the face of deficits, districts may be forced to end special programs and lay off staff.

EXAMPLE

This is an overview of the 2014/2015 budget for School District No. 41 (Burnaby).[3]

Revenue

In the 2014/2015 school year, School District No. 41 (Burnaby)—a large urban school district with 50 schools, more than 2000 employees, and 23 000 students—had revenue of $209 million, broken down as follows.

Budget Item	Revenue (in millions of $)
BC Ministry of Education operating grants	182.8
Other Ministry of Education grants	7.2
Other provincial/federal grants	0.4
Other fees and revenue	17.0
Rentals and leases	1.0
Investment income	0.9
Total	209.2

Expenses

The district spent more than 90 per cent of the overall budget on staff salaries and benefits. The expenses were broken down as follows.

Budget Item	Expenses (in millions of $)
Teacher salaries	102.5
Support staff salaries	32.8
Administrator salaries	8.5
Teachers on Call and other substitute staff salaries	6.2
Salaries of other professionals	3.8
Benefits for all school district employees	37.8
Supplies and services	22.4
Total	214.0

Note that the district's expenses add up to more than the district's revenue—in 2014/2015, School District No. 41 (Burnaby) had a budget shortfall of slightly less than $5 million. By law, school districts aren't allowed to carry deficits, so the district used a surplus it carried forward from the previous year to pay off the deficit.

Funding for Independent Schools

Independent schools are funded based on categories assigned by the BC Ministry of Education. The criteria for categorization of schools are outlined in the Classification of Independent Schools policy. For example, criteria include teacher certification. All independent schools in Groups 1 and 2 must have teachers certified by the Teacher Regulation Branch of the Ministry of Education, whereas schools in Groups 3 and 4 may have uncertified teachers.

A school may be classified in two groups for different portions of the school; for example, it may be in Group 1 for Kindergarten to Grade 7 and Group 3 for Grades 8 to 12.[4]

FUNDING FOR INDEPENDENT SCHOOLS[5]		
Group 1	**Group 2**	**Groups 3 and 4**
Schools receive 50 per cent of the per-pupil funding that public schools in the same district would receive.	Schools receive 35 per cent of the per-pupil funding that public schools in the same district would receive.	Schools do not receive funding from the Ministry of Education. They meet all of their expenses through tuition charges and fees.
Example: A Group 1 independent school in a district in which public schools receive $6900 per pupil would receive $3450.	Example: A Group 2 independent school in a district in which public schools receive $6900 per pupil would receive $2415.	

Khalsa School in Surrey is a Group 1 independent school that offers K–12 education with a focus on Sikh religion and cultural programs.

HOW GRADE LEVELS ARE ORGANIZED

British Columbia's school system is organized by grade level and is referred to as the *K–12 system* (Kindergarten to Grade 12).

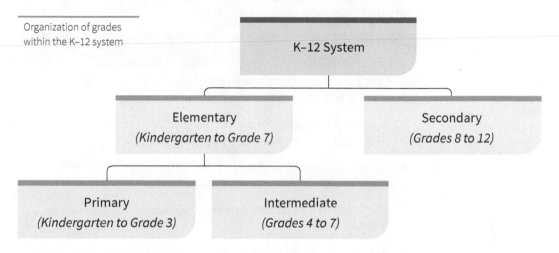

Organization of grades within the K–12 system

K–12 System

Elementary
(Kindergarten to Grade 7)

Secondary
(Grades 8 to 12)

Primary
(Kindergarten to Grade 3)

Intermediate
(Grades 4 to 7)

Each school board determines how schools are organized in the district, and the school configurations vary across the province. Examples of school configurations include elementary (K to Grade 7) and secondary (Grades 8 to 12); and elementary (K to Grade 5), middle (Grades 6 to 8), and secondary (Grades 9 to 12).

Elementary Education

Childhood development plays a role in the division of elementary education at the primary and intermediate levels. Instruction is designed to meet children's developmental needs at the different stages.

Primary Level: Kindergarten to Grade 3

Children in the primary grades learn through play and academics. These years provide a strong foundation of literacy and numeracy, and focus on developing socially appropriate skills such as problem solving, working with others, and self-regulation. Students are not evaluated with letter grades but through the use of **performance standards**. (See Part 5 on pages 93–101 for more information on assessment and evaluation.)

performance standard: a description of levels of achievement with respect to what students are expected to know and understand

As students progress through the primary grades, they begin to receive instruction in subjects such as language arts, social studies, mathematics, and science. Frequently these disciplines are not taught as discrete subjects, but rather through thematic units that integrate multiple subjects.

EXAMPLE

A Grade 2 class may complete a unit of study focusing on salmon, integrating science, social studies, and other subjects.

- Science is a key component as they examine the various stages of the salmon's life cycle and its environment.

- Social studies may be incorporated by looking at the significance of salmon to different cultures.

- Math may be incorporated by counting and measuring salmon fry.

- Students may be asked to draw or paint images of salmon to incorporate art into the unit of study.

- Language arts and issues of social responsibility may be addressed by having students write about their own personal beliefs about the importance of salmon and the need to protect its habitat.

This unit can be particularly meaningful for students because it provides hands-on learning experiences that extend beyond the classroom.

Intermediate Level: Grades 4 to 7

During the intermediate years, students are provided instruction in a variety of subjects such as

- English language arts (oral language, reading and viewing, writing and representing)
- arts education (dance, drama, visual arts, music)
- health and career education
- mathematics
- physical education (including daily physical activity)
- science
- social studies
- French as a second language

Beginning in Grade 4, students receive traditional letter grades. (See Part 5 on pages 93–101 for more information on assessment and evaluation.)

Secondary Level: Grades 8 to 12

In Grades 8 and 9, students usually take eight courses a year. Some courses are required. Others, called **elective courses**, are taken by choice. The required courses include

- English
- social studies
- math
- science
- physical education
- French as a second language (with some exceptions)

Students may also choose one or two elective courses, such as drama, technology education, or home economics.

In Grade 10, students begin the **Graduation Program**. They must successfully complete a number of required and elective courses, after which they receive the **BC Certificate of Graduation (Dogwood Diploma)**. (See page 35 for more information about graduation requirements.)

elective course: a course that is not mandatory but does contribute course credits

Graduation Program: the courses required to obtain the BC Certificate of Graduation (Dogwood Diploma)

BC Certificate of Graduation (Dogwood Diploma): granted by the BC Ministry of Education upon completion of the Graduation Program

BC students must earn a minimum of 80 course credits to receive a Dogwood Diploma.

PART 1

HOW THE SCHOOL SYSTEM WORKS

professional development day: a day during which teachers focus on developing skills and practices related to teaching; students do not attend school; also called *pro-D day*

HOW THE SCHOOL YEAR IS ORGANIZED

Schools and school districts set schedules for the school year based on criteria established by the Ministry of Education. These include the length of the school day, and the dates of most **professional development days**, vacation periods, early dismissals, and other days when school is not in session.

The typical elementary school day is structured as follows:

- Class starts between 8:30 a.m. and 9:00 a.m. and ends between 2:30 p.m. and 3:00 p.m.
- The day includes a 15-minute recess and a lunch break between 40 and 60 minutes in length.

Secondary schools have more variation in their instructional hours. Most students attend class from 8:30 a.m. to 3:15 p.m, but some schools offer classes between 7:30 a.m. and 4:30 p.m.

Individual schools and districts have some flexibility in organizing their instructional hours and calendars, which is done in consultation with parents, schools, and partner groups (including teachers). The school board and the BC Ministry of Education must approve the calendar.

By law, schools must be in session for a minimum of 180 days, although this number varies slightly from year to year; schools are often in session for up to 190 days. There can be no more than six professional days in a school year. Students must receive the following minimum hours of instruction per year:

- Kindergarten: 853 hours
- Grades 1 to 7: 878 hours
- Grades 8 to 12: 952 hours[6]

linear system: a school calendar in which the same courses are taught throughout the year

semester system: a system used in secondary schools in which the school calendar is divided into two halves called semesters, with students taking half of their yearly courses in each semester of the school year

School Calendar: Linear Versus Semester

Schools' annual calendars are structured using one of two systems: linear or semester. Some districts offer only one type of system district-wide, while larger districts may offer both systems. In some schools, a blend between linear and semester programs is offered to provide a variety of learning opportunities.

Within the linear and semester systems, there are multiple variations of the timetables; the following explanations provide common examples.

Linear System

Most elementary and middle schools use a linear system or some variation of it. The year is divided into three terms of approximately 60 days of instruction, with a formal report card issued at the end of each term. Students' courses remain the same throughout the school year.

EXAMPLE

This is a sample timetable for a Grade 7 student in an elementary school on a linear system.

Time	Monday	Tuesday	Wednesday	Thursday	Friday
9:00–9:45	Class meeting	Music	Language arts	Language arts	Physical education
9:45–10:30	Physical education	Social studies	Social studies	Social studies	Music
10:30–10:45	Recess				
10:45–11:30	Math	Math	Assembly	Math	Math
11:30–12:00	Science	Science	Math	Science	Science
12:00–12:40	Lunch				
12:40–1:00	Silent reading	Silent reading	Silent reading	Silent reading	Silent reading
1:00–1:45	Language arts	Computers	Physical education	Library	Band
1:45–2:30	French as a second language	French as a second language	Music	French as a second language	Health and career education
2:30–2:45	Planner and cleanup	Planner and cleanup	Planner and cleanup	Planner and cleanup	Planner and cleanup

In the linear system at the secondary level, students typically take eight courses a year—four classes one day (Day 1) and the other four the next (Day 2). As in elementary schools, secondary schools provide formal report cards at the end of each term.

This is a sample timetable for a Grade 10 student in a secondary school following a linear system.

Time	Day 1	Day 2
Block A: 8:40–9:50	Social Studies 10	Science 10
Class change/Break		
Block B: 10:15–11:25	Physical Education 10	Planning 10
Lunch		
Block C: 12:25–1:35	Math 10	English 10
Class change		
Block D: 1:45–2:55	Home Economics 10	Drama 10
Exams (take place in June): Science 10, Math 10, English 10		

Semester System

In the semester system, the year is divided into two segments of approximately 90 days of instruction. Typically, Semester 1 is from September to the end of January, Semester 2 is from February to the end of June, and students take four courses each semester. Report cards are issued in the middle and at the end of each semester.

This is a sample timetable for a Grade 10 student in a secondary school following a semester system.

Time	Semester 1 (September–January)	Semester 2 (February–June)
Block A: 9:00–10:17	Science 10	Math 10
Class change		
Block B: 10:22–11:43	Drama 10	English 10
Lunch		
Block C: 12:23–1:40	Planning 10	Physical Education 10
Class change		
Block D: 1:45–3:02	Social Studies 10	Home Economics 10
	Exam (end of January): Science 10	**Exams (June):** Math 10, English 10

Advantages and Disadvantages to Linear/Semester Systems

Each calendar system has advantages and disadvantages.

Linear System	Semester System
Students take up to eight courses at a time, which can increase stress for some students.	Students take only four classes at a time, which may reduce stress for some students.
Students take all courses through the entire school year, ensuring continuity of subject matter. For example, the most time off that a student has between Math 9 and Math 10 is two months (summer).	Students may have a long gap between courses in the same subject matter and struggle to retain information. For example, a student can take Math 9 in the first semester of Grade 9 and Math 10 in the second semester of Grade 10, resulting in a full year between the two courses.
Students who are absent from class miss less course content than students missing the same number of school days in a semester system.	The course material is covered over a condensed time period (although with approximately the same amount of class time) compared to the linear system.
Students have as many as four exams at the end of the school year.	Student take a maximum of two exams at any given time.
International Baccalaureate and Advanced Placement courses are offered. (See pages 62–63 for details about these programs.)	International Baccalaureate and Advanced Placement courses are not compatible with the semester calendar.
Breaks/exam periods are not scheduled between terms.	Students have a short break between semesters, attending school only to complete exams and assignments.
Teachers have designated preparation time throughout the school year.	Teachers teach fewer classes and students at a time. However, since they teach seven blocks a year, teachers who teach four classes in the first semester and three in the second go nearly five months without any designated preparation time.

THE PROVINCIAL CURRICULUM

In British Columbia, the Ministry of Education's curriculum department sets the standards for all courses from Kindergarten through Grade 12. Curriculum is contained in modules known as Integrated Resource Packages (IRP). IRPs include Prescribed Learning Outcomes (PLOs), suggested resources, and assessment strategies. They are public documents available on the ministry's website so that teachers, parents, and students can see the requirements both before selecting a course (as in secondary school) and while students are enrolled in a program of study. PLOs can help parents to understand the learning activities in which their children are engaged and how they relate to the IRP.

curriculum: the content that is prescribed in a course

Integrated Resource Package (IRP): curriculum document that includes Prescribed Learning Outcomes, teaching strategies, assessment tools, and resources

Prescribed Learning Outcomes (PLOs): the specific knowledge, skills, or abilities that students must be able to demonstrate by the end of each course and grade level

EXAMPLE

The Grade 4 Science curriculum indicates students are expected to "measure weather in terms of temperature, precipitation, cloud cover, wind speed and direction." [7]

The English Language Arts Curriculum for Grade 11 (commonly known as English 11) states that students are expected to "interpret, analyse, and evaluate ideas and information from texts, by

- critiquing logic and quality of evidence

- relating and critiquing perspectives

- identifying and challenging bias, contradictions, and distortions

- identifying the importance and impact of social, political, and historical contexts"[8]

The curriculum undergoes cycles of development, design, consultation, and implementation approximately once every decade. The BC Ministry of Education explains that "curriculum development is an ongoing process informed by research and global trends."[9] New curriculum for Kindergarten to Grade 9 will be implemented in September 2015. Curriculum for Grades 10 to 12 is currently in development. The redesigned curriculum will emphasize key concepts, core competencies, and skills needed in the 21st century.[10]

Graduation Requirements

The **Graduation Transitions Program** is a component of the provincial curriculum designed to ensure students have carefully considered and made plans for their life after secondary school. Students earn 4 **course credits** by completing the program's Prescribed Learning Outcomes in a classroom setting or through independent study.

To successfully complete the requirements of the BC Certificate of Graduation, students must achieve the Prescribed Learning Outcomes of the following courses and earn 80 course credits from the Grade 10 level or higher.[11]

Graduation requirements

GRADE 10	• a Language Arts 10 • a Social Studies 10 • a Science 10	• a Mathematics 10 • Physical Education 10 • Planning 10
GRADE 11	• a Language Arts 11 • a Social Studies 11 (or 12)	• a Science 11 (or 12) • a Mathematics 11 (or 12)
GRADE 12	• a Language Arts 12	• Graduation Transitions Program
GRADE 10, 11, OR 12	**A FINE ARTS &/OR APPLIED SKILLS COURSE**	
	• fine arts include music, drama, dance, and art	• applied skills include business education, home economics, and technology education
ELECTIVES	• 28 course credits	

It is worth noting that a student taking a full course load of eight courses a year in Grades 10 to 12 will graduate with 96 credits or more. This permits students a broad learning experience and also builds in some flexibility for senior students who may choose to take a reduced course load. It also allows for students who may not have completed a course to retake it and still graduate on time.

Graduation Transitions Program: a required course that includes post-secondary planning, careers research, and healthy living planning

course credit: a number value assigned to a course as a measure of progress toward completion of a program, such as the BC Certificate of Graduation

Note: These graduation requirements are accurate at the time of publication of this book. However, it is important to note the BC Ministry of Education may change graduation requirements at any time. Your child should check with the school's counsellor to ensure that his or her courses meet current ministry requirements.

SCHOOL BUS

EMERGENCY EXIT

SCHOOL BUS

CHOOL BUS

EMERGE

PART 2

Choosing a School

KEY QUESTIONS

- What makes a good school *good*? How can you tell if your child's school is a good school?

- How can you choose the right public school for your child? What factors should you consider?

- Is an independent school the right choice for your child? What factors should you consider?

- Once you've chosen a school, how do you enroll your child?

WHAT MAKES A GOOD SCHOOL *GOOD*?

International studies have shown that British Columbia's public school system is one of the best, most highly functional systems in the world.[1] Most parents in the province do choose to take advantage of our excellent public schools, but there are a great many different schools to choose from within the public and independent systems. So how do you choose? Which school is right for your child?

Schools are more than just a number on a ranking list, a description on a website, or a collection of rooms and desks, teachers, and students. They are living things that have an atmosphere, a feeling, and, some would say, a soul. You can often walk into a school and intuitively get a good feeling about the place without truly understanding why.

But what creates these feelings? What makes a good school *good* and how can you tell? What sort of things do you look for? What sort of questions do you ask?

What Effective Schools Do by Lawrence W. Lezotte and Kathleen McKee Snyder provides parents and educators with some powerful tools to help determine what makes a good school and if your neighbourhood school fits the criteria. In short, good schools

- are safe and organized learning environments
- set high expectations for students
- have strong leadership
- have a clear mission[2]

How to Identify a Good School

You can get a sense about the quality of a school before you even walk through the front doors. Do the members of the community respect the building? Is it clean or is there garbage on the grounds? Does the place look well maintained or run down? Does it look like the students and staff take pride in their school?

Walk through the school entrance toward the principal's office. As you walk the hallways, what do you observe? Do you see students engaged in their work? Are their work and accomplishments proudly displayed on the classroom walls?

> *The effective school is built on a foundation of high expectations, strong leadership, unwavering commitment to learning for all, collaboration, differentiated instruction, and frequent monitoring of student progress.*
>
> —Lezotte & McKee Snyder, 2011[3]

When you get to the office, how are you greeted? When you ask to speak with the principal, what is the response? Good principals make time to meet with parents, but keep in mind that it may be best to make an appointment to meet with them since they are often out of the office working with students and teachers.

When the meeting with the principal takes place, what is your sense of it? Are you made to feel welcome? Focus your questions for the principal on the four tenets of a good school as outlined by Lezotte and McKee Snyder. The following suggestions will help you get a good idea about the school and the people who lead it.

- **Ask about the learning environment.**

  What is the school's **code of conduct**? Is it displayed in the school for all to see? How does the principal deal with issues such as bullying? How does the school meet students' learning needs? What supports are available for students who require learning assistance?

- **Ask about the expectations for students.**

  What goals are students expected to achieve? A good school—regardless of size or type—sets high academic standards for its students. How is student learning monitored to ensure that everyone succeeds?

- **Ask yourself about the school leadership.**

  Does the principal seem passionate about the job, and know the students and their families? Does he or she explain what is good about the school and what improvements the school community is working to achieve? Does the principal have a vision for what the school is and what it can be, and does he or she engage members of the school community in implementing that vision?

- **Ask about the school's mission and goals.**

  What is the school's mission, and is it displayed in the school? Is the school community working on any school-wide goals? Such goals tend to be academic (for example, improving reading or math skills) and social-emotional (such as teaching students self-regulation or improving their citizenship skills).

  Ask why those goals were chosen, and what data was used to set them. What progress has the school made in meeting those goals? What are the next steps?

code of conduct: a document that outlines the behavioural expectations for students in a school

PART 2

CHOOSING A SCHOOL

HOW TO CHOOSE A PUBLIC SCHOOL

By understanding what to look for in a good school, you can choose a suitable school for your child. You may apply to enroll your child in any public school in the province, but school districts can set procedures and policies to prioritize placement of students (described in more detail on pages 44–46).

The first place to start your search is on the school district website. If you live in a larger school district with many schools, the district website should include either a map of each school's **catchment area** or an online school locator tool for finding your neighbourhood school. The website also provides basic information about each school, such as the address and contact information, number of students, and administration, and a link to the school's website (if applicable).

catchment area: the area defined by the school district as being served by a particular school

The school's website should provide more details about the school, for example, its goals, school plan, mission statement, and programs. Secondary schools in particular have a significant amount of information on their websites. There may also be links to specific departments or teachers' contact information and their class web pages.

You can also learn a great deal about a school on the Ministry of Education's website. Depending on whether you are looking at a secondary or elementary school, this website provides data on

- school demographics
- provincial exam results
- Foundation Skills Assessment results (see page 99 for more information about this assessment)
- graduation rates
- transition rates from grade to grade
- satisfaction survey results
- class sizes

When choosing a school for your child, visit the school, ask the questions suggested on page 39, and consider how the following factors may affect your decision.

- **Programs or schools of choice**

  Some schools offer specific academic, language, or athletic programs that may be right for your child. Part 3 of this book describes these options in depth.

- **School size**

  Some parents like the community experience in a smaller school, while others prefer the opportunities a larger school can offer their child. Student population can vary greatly between school in a district. For example, the largest elementary school in School District No. 37 (Delta) is Sunshine Hills Elementary, with nearly 600 students, while one of the district's smallest schools, English Bluff Elementary, has fewer than 200 students.

- **After-school programs**

  Some schools offer a number of after-school activities for students. Community schools (described on page 60) are often busy until late in the evening with athletic, academic, and artistic programs for students as well as for community members.

- **Child care**

  Child care before and after school can be difficult to find. Daycare that is available either on site or immediately adjacent to the school can make a parent's life much easier.

- **Reputation**

  Word of mouth, media coverage, and the Fraser Institute rankings (see page 42) all contribute to a school's reputation. However, reputation should not be the single deciding factor in your choice of school. Whether the school meets your child's needs should be the most important consideration in your decision.

Ultimately, selecting a school comes down to a combination of factors, such as proximity to home, personal choice, and the programs available. If you do your research and ask the right questions, you can find the ideal school for your child.

Foundation Skills Assessment (FSA): a standardized test given to BC students in Grades 4 and 7

Consider a number of factors when choosing a school for your child, including what types of extracurricular activities are available.

FRASER INSTITUTE SCHOOL RANKING

The Fraser Institute, an independent research and educational organization with no affiliation with the BC Ministry of Education, publishes an annual School Report Card that ranks schools on a scale of one to ten.

The rankings are based on a number of factors, including the results of the Foundation Skills Assessment (FSA) tests for students in Grades 4 and 7 (see page 99 for more information about the tests), provincial exam marks, and other school and demographic data.

Many parents wonder whether the school ranking should influence their choice of school. This question is understandable given that the methods and purpose of the school ranking are the subject of considerable debate and controversy.

To learn more about how the rankings are created and about the Fraser Institute's methodology and purpose, the following sources may be helpful:

- Fraser Institute: www.fraserinstitute.org

- "Ending the Reign of the Fraser Institute's School Rankings" by Helen Raptis, published in the *Canadian Journal of Education* (2013, volume 35, pages 187–201), accessible at: http://journals .sfu.ca/cje/index.php/cje-rce/article/download/864/1167

HOW TO ENROLL YOUR CHILD IN THE PUBLIC SCHOOL OF YOUR CHOICE

Once you've chosen a school for your child, what are the next steps? This section provides information about how to enroll your child in a BC public school.

Registering at Your Neighbourhood Public School

If you choose to send your child to the neighbourhood school, the registration process is relatively simple. School districts open registration for September around February of the same calendar year, and parents are usually required to visit the school to begin the registration process. Check your school district's website for district-specific information.

If you move into the community in the middle of the school year, visit the school in person to register. If the school is full, the principal will direct you to the school district office where staff will talk to you about your child's schooling options. If you know in advance that you are going to move, be sure to contact the new school in the neighbourhood as soon as possible to let them know that you are arriving.

In some districts, the registration process is completed with pen and paper, while in others it is done online. Regardless of the format, a significant amount of personal information about the parent(s) and child is required.

EXAMPLE

School District No. 44 (North Vancouver) requires the following documents to register new students:

- birth certificate (if not born in Canada, proof of citizenship or permanent residency)
- proof of current address (such as a utility bill)
- proof of guardianship, if applicable
- report card from previous school, if applicable
- completed registration form, which includes information about medical and special learning considerations[4]

Carefully following registration procedures will help make your child's first day at a new school a positive experience.

Why is so much information required? Schools have an obligation to ensure

- the child is who the parent says he or she is
- the parents are who they say they are and that they have legal custody of the child
- the child has the necessary residency rights to attend a BC public school

Registering at a Public School from Outside the Catchment Area

For children in rural and northern areas of the province, there may be no choice in schools. Many communities have only one elementary school and one secondary school, or one school that serves the entire student body from Kindergarten to Grade 12. For families in larger urban and suburban school districts, however, the public school options are numerous. Some families, for a variety of reasons, choose schools in different neighbourhoods or school districts from where they live.

If you decide that you would like your child to attend a non-neighbourhood school, the process for registering is similar to that of your neighbourhood school. Parents do have the right to apply for a spot for their child in any public school, but school districts can set policies to prioritize placement of students.

EXAMPLE

School District No. 23 (Central Okanagan) prioritizes student placement as follows:[5]

Catchment area students who, in the previous year, attended the school

Catchment area students who, in the previous year, were placed by the district in a different school

Siblings of catchment area students

New students in the catchment area

Siblings of students from outside the catchment area who are currently enrolled in the school

Students from outside the catchment area but within the district

Students from outside the school district

International students

If you are interested in registering your child in a school from outside its catchment area, go to the school district website (follow the links under keywords such as "Parents" or "Registration") and review the specific rules for that district. Generally, once your child has been accepted into a school, he or she can stay there regardless of where you live. You can improve your chances of securing a space for your child by meeting registration deadlines. Often the demand for spots in certain public schools far exceeds the supply.

There may be additional factors that can help you register your child in your school of choice. Ensure that you give every legitimate reason as to why you want your child to attend that particular school. For example, in some school districts, child care close to the school is a factor in deciding placement. It can also be useful to talk to the principal of the school you would like your child to attend.

If your initial attempt is unsuccessful, register your child in your neighbourhood school, determine the waitlist process for your school of choice, and ensure that your child is on that waitlist.

When choosing your child's school, consider transportation. If you live outside the catchment area, will your child be eligible for school bus transportation?

HOW TO CHOOSE AN INDEPENDENT SCHOOL

Thirteen per cent of BC's school-aged children—about 80 000 students—are enrolled in the province's more than 330 independent schools.[6] The BC Ministry of Education regulates independent schools through the *Independent School Act* and the *School Act*.

Whether you want your child to attend a school that focuses on religious values, university preparation, special needs, or a particular educational philosophy, there is a BC independent school to meet your needs. The independent system includes day schools and boarding schools; small, intimate schools and large K–12 schools; and schools open to only boys or girls. The following types of independent schools can be found across British Columbia:

- **Religious schools**

  If it important that your child's education be infused with religious values, there are many faith-based schools to choose from, including Christian, Islamic, Sikh, and Jewish schools. Examples include St. Patrick Regional Secondary School in Vancouver, BC Muslim School in Richmond, Khalsa School in Surrey, and Vancouver Hebrew Academy.

- **Cultural and/or language schools**

  Some independent schools focus on imparting specific cultural knowledge and traditions. Examples include independent schools operated by First Nations communities, such as Acwsalcta School in Bella Coola, and French schools such as French International School Cousteau, which meets the requirements of both the BC Ministry of Education and the French Ministry of Education.

- **University preparatory schools**

  These schools are modelled after the British university preparatory schools and have a reputation for high academic standards. Preparatory schools are often able to offer a variety of extracurricular activities, such as arts and sports. Examples include Crofton House School and St. George's School in Vancouver, Brentwood College in Mill Bay, and Shawnigan Lake School in Shawnigan Lake.

gifted: a designation given to students with specific, above-average strengths in cognitive areas

- **Schools for students with special needs**

  Many independent schools focus on students with special needs, such as a learning disability or giftedness. Schools that focus on programs for students with learning disabilities and challenges include Fraser Academy in Vancouver; the Eaton Arrowsmith Schools in Vancouver, White Rock, and Victoria; Discovery School in Victoria; and the Kenneth Gordon Maplewood School in North Vancouver. Schools for gifted students include Madrona Independent School in Vancouver and Choice School in Richmond.

- **Schools with specific educational philosophies**

  Independent schools may embrace particular teaching methods or approaches, such as Montessori, Reggio Emilia, or Waldorf. (See pages 70–71 for more information about Montessori and Reggio Emilia.) Examples include Maria Montessori Academy in Victoria; York House School in Vancouver, which bases its Kindergarten programs on the Reggio Emilia approach; and Cedar Valley Waldorf School in Squamish.

You may wish to consider the following factors when deciding whether to enroll your child in an independent school:

Choice School for the Gifted and Exceptional in Richmond emphasizes academic excellence and life-skills development.

- **Tuition**

  The BC government subsidizes many independent schools, but the schools do charge tuition and the range is vast. For example, Khalsa School charges approximately $1100 to $1600, while Shawnigan Lake School charges about $44000 a year for tuition and board.[7] Schools may offer subsidies or scholarships to help fund your child's education.

- **Location**

  Is transportation provided? Consider the time and expense of transporting your child to and from school activities and social events.

Visit the website of the school you are considering and speak with its admissions staff to learn more about the school's values, strengths, and program options to help you make the most informed decision for your child.

HOW TO ENROLL YOUR CHILD IN THE INDEPENDENT SCHOOL OF YOUR CHOICE

Most independent schools have an application process: potential students apply for admission and are evaluated on a number of criteria before being invited to register. Each independent school's application procedure is different, and you will need to find out about their individual requirements from their website or a visit to their office. Some, especially the university preparatory schools, have a rigorous application process that can vary depending on the age of the child.

EXAMPLE

St. Michaels University School in Victoria has different application criteria for Kindergarten, Grades 1 to 3, Grades 4 and 5, Grades 6 to 12, and English Language Learners. For example, parents applying to enroll their child in Grades 6 to 12 are required to complete a three-part application process:

1. Parents complete the online application form, providing documentation such as a birth certificate, student records, and so on.

2. The admissions team reviews the applications and invites selected candidates to the school, where they write an entrance test, attend an interview, and tour the campus.

3. After the testing and the campus visit, the admissions team reviews the candidates once again. Afterwards, candidates either receive an offer of placement, a spot on the waitlist, or a non-acceptance decision. A student is not accepted when staff members either feel that there is no room in a particular grade or do not consider the student to be a good fit for the school.

In addition, there is a non-refundable $250 application fee, and successful applicants pay a one-time non-refundable registration fee of $2000 or $2500, depending on whether the student will live on or off the school grounds.

For the 2015/2016 school year, BC students in Grades 9 to 12 living off campus are charged about $20 000 a year in tuition, while those living in residence pay over $45 000 a year for tuition, room, and board. The cost is nearly $60 000 for international students.[8]

PART 3

Program and Schooling Options

KEY QUESTIONS

- What program and schooling options are available for your child?

- What are the benefits of each option?

- Is one of these options the right choice for your child?

  - homeschooling
  - distributed learning
  - francophone schools
  - French immersion
  - other language immersion programs
  - community schools
  - Advanced Placement program
  - International Baccalaureate program
  - Aboriginal education programs
  - arts programs
  - sports programs
  - Montessori and Reggio Emilia programs
  - challenge programs
  - multi-age cluster classes
  - vocational programs
  - other programs of choice

WHAT PROGRAM AND SCHOOLING OPTIONS ARE AVAILABLE?

At one time, *choice* was not a word associated with education. It was taken for granted that parents would enroll their children in the neighbourhood public school, where they would stay until their graduation. But there are now hundreds of independent schools in the province competing for students and, in the public system, parents have the right to enroll their child in any school in any district if space is available.

In many of BC's school districts, public schools offer programs for gifted and highly academic students, students with musical or artistic talents or athletic ability, and students who want to focus on culture and language studies. Programs can be tailored specifically for elementary or secondary students, or for all grade levels. They may be offered in a variety of settings, including the neighbourhood school, a separate facility, or online. Some programs are offered in every school in the district, while others only in select schools where enrollment requires transfer out of the neighbourhood school.

Not all schools and districts have the same ability to offer programs of choice. That said, technology has made it possible to offer more choices to more students, even in the most remote schools. This part of the book provides an overview of the most popular schools and programs of choice in British Columbia.

Norgate Community School in School District No. 44 (North Vancouver) offers programs for students and adults in the community, including active play, Squamish language, and resumé writing.

HOMESCHOOLING

One option parents might consider is not sending their children to school at all. Section 12 of the *School Act* gives you the legal right to educate your child at home. **Homeschooling** allows you to select which subjects to teach your child, in both the manner and on a timeline of your choice. Homeschooling does not have to follow the ministry curriculum and government officials do not monitor student learning. In British Columbia, about 2000 children are homeschooled.[1]

homeschooling: teaching children at home without the supervision of a certified teacher

Is Homeschooling the Right Choice for Your Child?

Some common reasons parents choose homeschooling include
- a desire to strengthen the family unit by keeping children at home
- philosophical or religious differences about what is taught in schools or how it is taught
- a desire to assert parental responsibility over their children's education[2]

If any of these reasons resonate with you, then perhaps homeschooling is an option to consider. There are some challenges and consequences associated with homeschooling that you should take into consideration:
- Your child may miss out on the interaction with other children that can enhance social and emotional development.
- Your child will not receive a BC Certificate of Graduation (Dogwood Diploma) unless he or she enrolls in secondary school by Grade 10. (This can include distributed learning; see page 54.)
- You must have the skills and the time necessary to provide an education to your child.

If you choose homeschooling, you must register (but not enroll) your child at a school for him or her to be considered a legitimate homeschooled student. Registration also makes two resources available:
- access to assessment and evaluation by school staff (evaluation is only conducted at your request)
- the loan of school resources to help support your child's educational program

DISTRIBUTED LEARNING

distributed learning: learning that does not require face-to-face interaction; can be done over the Internet or through direct distribution of course material

Distributed learning (also called *online learning* or *distance learning*) is available as an enhancement or alternative to regular schooling. It is available for K–12 students in every district in the province. More than 48 000 school-aged students in British Columbia are enrolled in distributed learning programs.[3]

How distance learning is offered is determined by the evaluation needs (such as a required provincial examination) or the distance a student may live from a school or learning centre. The following are some of the models offered:

- Students may submit all of their coursework via the Internet and go to a school only for tests or examinations.
- Students may participate in a blend of online learning and face-to-face meetings with the teacher. They may submit their assignments online and correspond with their teachers through email or by telephone or video conferencing.
- Students may start and complete courses following a linear or semester calendar, or they may participate in a program that offers continuous entry, allowing them to begin a course at any time.

Homeschooling and distributed learning may seem similar, but there are significant differences. While the Ministry of Education does not supervise or monitor homeschooled students, students enrolled in a distributed learning program receive support from a certified teacher, are taught the BC curriculum, and graduate with a BC Certificate of Graduation (Dogwood Diploma) upon successful completion of their studies.

Students in distributed learning programs may need parental support and encouragement to be successful. The completion rate for courses in Grades 8 to 12 is approximately 66 per cent.[4]

Is Distributed Learning the Right Choice for Your Child?

The reasons students enroll in distributed learning are as varied as the students themselves:

- Some students take distributed learning courses while attending regular school, often in order to take advantage of courses not offered at their school.
- Students with health conditions or physical limitations that prevent them from attending regular school may find that distributed learning better meets their needs.
- Students living overseas may enroll in distributed learning to maintain a connection to their home district.

Distributed learning is used by students who need the flexibility and variety the program provides, or who feel they just don't "fit in" at regular schools. Some students take a number of courses at the same time, while others focus on a single course for several weeks, and then move on to the next course.

If you are considering distributed learning options for your child, keep in mind these possible challenges:

- There are minimum computer and network requirements to participate in an online distributed learning program.
- If your child has difficulty with self-motivation, he or she may struggle without the structure of the classroom.
- If your child has learning disabilities, this program may not meet his or her learning needs. Teachers have difficulty providing over the Internet the level of support students with learning disabilities require.

PART 3

PROGRAM AND SCHOOLING OPTIONS

EXAMPLE

BC Online School is a division of Kelowna's Heritage Christian Online School. It is an independent school that offers education with a Christian perspective to all students in the province at no cost—the Ministry of Education pays the tuition. Their course offerings cover subjects as diverse as Bible studies, robotics, calculus, video gaming, and screenwriting.[5]

FRANCOPHONE SCHOOLS

Conseil scolaire francophone de la Colombie-Britannique (CSF): the public school district responsible for schools that offer French as the primary language of instruction for students whose first language is French

French is one of Canada's official languages and francophone parents have minority language rights under the *Canadian Charter of Rights and Freedoms* to have their children educated in French. The Conseil scolaire francophone de la Colombie-Britannique (CSF) offers French as the primary language of instruction at nearly 40 schools throughout the province. The CSF schools follow the BC curriculum and differ from French immersion schools in that students are expected to speak French as a *first* language. The CSF (also known as the Francophone Education Authority or School District No. 93) is the school district of choice for more than 5000 BC students whose first language is French.[6]

Is a Francophone School the Right Choice for Your Child?

Your child is eligible for admission to a francophone school if he or she meets one of the following criteria:

- His or her first language is French and he or she still understands French.
- One of your child's parents received primary schooling in French in Canada (excluding immersion).
- One of your child's parents has a child who received or is receiving primary or secondary schooling in French in Canada (excluding immersion).[7]

The admissions committee of the CSF may also consider admission of your child if he or she has

- a parent who is an immigrant who received primary schooling in French or who understands and speaks French fluently
- a grandparent who is a Canadian citizen or permanent resident whose first language is French or who received primary or secondary schooling in French (excluding immersion)[8]

Part of the schools' mandate is to promote francophone language and culture. If you enroll your child in a CSF school, you will be encouraged to participate in the francophone community. It is important to note that, in this school system, the school and the CSF communicate with parents primarily in French.

FRENCH IMMERSION

There is no doubt that, of all programs of choice offered in the public school system, the **French immersion program** is the most popular. In 2014/2015, about 51 000 students—or 8 per cent of students enrolled in K–12 schools—were in French immersion.[9] Competition to register in the program is often intense. Many families enter lotteries for space or line up overnight to register their children in one of the coveted spots.

But what exactly is French immersion and what is the reason for its popularity? According to the BC Ministry of Education,

> the major goal of French Immersion is to provide the opportunity for non-francophone students to become bilingual in English and French. Bilingualism is achieved by providing instruction of the basic curriculum entirely in French during the first years. Once a firm base in French has been established, instruction in English language arts is added, and instruction in the English language gradually increases. Students continue to receive instruction in certain subjects in French so that proficiency is achieved in both languages by the end of Grade 12.[10]

There are two streams of French immersion offered in the school system. In both models, students are taught the same BC curriculum as students in non-French immersion schools.

French immersion program: a program in which French is taught as a second language, but is the primary language of instruction

PART 3

PROGRAM AND SCHOOLING OPTIONS

EARLY FRENCH IMMERSION	LATE FRENCH IMMERSION
• Begins in Kindergarten or Grade 1 • Proportion of instruction in French: ‣ Kindergarten to Grade 3: 100% ‣ Grades 4 to 7: 80%, with English gradually introduced	• Begins in Grade 6 • Proportion of instruction in French: ‣ Grade 6: 100% ‣ Grade 7: 80%

SECONDARY SCHOOL
Proportion of French instruction decreases gradually to 25% in Grades 11 and 12

French immersion program streams[11]

Is French Immersion the Right Choice for Your Child?

There are many benefits of learning a second language:[12]

- Bilingual students score higher in verbal and non-verbal intelligence, reading, language, and mathematics.
- Students learning a second language often see improved language skills in their first language.
- Students studying a second language are more culturally sensitive and adapt better to different cultures.
- People who are bilingual may have increased employment opportunities.

The language benefits are clear, but you should be aware that there are some challenges and additional costs that come with the French immersion program. Consider the following:

- **How will your child get to school?**
  Since it is your responsibility to provide transportation to and from the program, the time and expense of transportation should be considered.
- **How will your child's social network be affected?**
  Attending school in a different neighbourhood has the potential to impact your child's friendships in the neighbourhood. Consider the implications in time and expense of travel for play dates, sleepovers, school functions, and other social events.
- **Does it meet the needs of your child?**
  Your child's needs and wants should be considered strongly in this decision. Even at five or six years of age, a child's personality and temperament have started to develop and you should have a good idea about whether or not French immersion would be a good fit. Your child's participation in the decision when he or she is older is critical. Enrolling your child in late immersion against his or her will can result in argument and conflict.
- **Will you be satisfied if your child does not become fully bilingual?**
  Like anything, the more you put into the program, the more you get out of it, and many students in immersion are fluent in French upon graduation. However, a large

number of students do not achieve fluency because they lose interest, don't put in the work required, don't have the time required because of commitments to extra-curricular activities, or simply don't have the aptitude to fully learn a second language.

- **Do you have the ability to support your child's schooling?** It isn't just the children who learn French when immersion is involved. In order to fully support their child, parents often have their own learning to do.

EXAMPLE

École Poirier Elementary School in School District No. 62 (Sooke) describes a successful immersion student as a child who

- is verbal and likes to talk
- shows strengths in his or her first language
- has good auditory discrimination
- has a good memory
- is usually attentive and focused
- readily accepts challenges
- self-corrects
- imitates easily
- trusts
- experiments without fear of making mistakes[13]

OTHER LANGUAGE IMMERSION PROGRAMS

Some districts offer immersion programs in languages other than French, including

- Mandarin: School District No. 39 (Vancouver), School District No. 41 (Burnaby), School District No. 43 (Coquitlam)
- Punjabi: School District No. 36 (Surrey)
- Russian: School District No. 20 (Kootenay-Columbia)

Check your school district's website to find out if your district offers any other language immersion programs.

COMMUNITY SCHOOLS

Typical schools operate from 8:00 a.m. to 4:00 p.m., Monday to Friday, and are vacant on weekends and holidays. While some do offer extracurricular programs or lease space to other organizations, they remain one of the most underutilized public resources in the province. Community schools are an exception to this pattern.

Community schools have the dedicated staffing and the mandate to work with government, service providers, private organizations, and individuals to provide programs for students and community members.

To find out if there is a community school in your neighbourhood, go to the website of your school district or the Association for Community Education in British Columbia (ACEbc), the organization that represents and supports community schools across the province. It has a comprehensive list of all community schools in the province as well as contact information.

community school: a school that offers programs when school is out of session and encourages the participation of community residents

Is a Community School the Right Choice for Your Child?

Community schools bring together education, services, activities, and programs to foster community engagement and involvement. Often, the schools include public health programs such as family counselling and drug and alcohol support. If you are looking for athletic, academic, arts, and wellness programs for your child, you may wish to consider the community school option.

EXAMPLE

Edmonds Community School in School District No. 41 (Burnaby) is an urban school of approximately 300 students, a significant number of whom are immigrants, refugees, and English Language Learners. In partnership with the school district, the city, non-profit and service groups, local business, and individuals, the school runs 30 programs that support the needs of the students and their families. These programs, almost all of which are offered at no or low cost to allow low-income families to participate, include a family literacy program run by the Canucks Family Education Centre, hip hop lessons run by a local dancing studio, and sports programs run by the City of Burnaby.[14]

ADVANCED PLACEMENT PROGRAM

The **Advanced Placement (AP) program** is a series of enrichment courses available in many secondary schools across the province. The primary appeal of AP is that, with successful completion of an AP course and its corresponding exam, a student can earn credit for a post-secondary course while still in secondary school. Students can take just one or multiple AP courses, depending on aptitude and availability of courses.

AP is managed by the College Board, a non-profit organization in New York. In British Columbia, more than 160 schools offer Advanced Placement courses in art, music, physics, biology, calculus, economics, history, and languages.[15]

Earning post-secondary credit depends on successful completion of the AP exam. Generally, exams are written in May of each year, are three hours in length, and include a combination of multiple choice, written, and oral responses. For subjects such as art, there is also a portfolio component. Performance on an AP exam is measured on a scale of 1 to 5.

> **Advanced Placement (AP) program**: courses designed to challenge students academically that may earn them credit for a post-secondary course

PART 3

PROGRAM AND SCHOOLING OPTIONS

Is the Advanced Placement Program the Right Choice for Your Child?

The Advanced Placement courses require a high degree of academic rigour and the program allows your child to choose courses in the subject areas of interest to him or her. If your child is interested in pursuing challenging learning opportunities and is willing to commit to the time and effort required, then the Advanced Placement program may be the right choice.

A student who successfully completes AP Chemistry may be eligible for credit for a first-year university chemistry course.

INTERNATIONAL BACCALAUREATE PROGRAM

International Baccalaureate (IB) program: an academically rigorous program that encourages students to develop global awareness

While no program in British Columbia is as popular as French immersion, the International Baccalaureate (IB) program has few equals in academic reputation. A non-profit educational organization founded in 1968 in Geneva, Switzerland, IB develops curriculum, evaluates and certifies schools across the globe that wish to offer its programs, and assesses students in the program. Currently more than 350 schools in Canada offer the IB program.[16]

IB's mission is to "develop inquiring, knowledgeable, and caring young people who help to create a better and more peaceful world through intercultural understanding and respect."[17] It offers four programs for students aged 3 to 19 as shown in the table on the opposite page. Each program usually incorporates the curriculum of the jurisdiction where it is offered, while focusing on specific themes.

Is the International Baccalaureate Program the Right Choice for Your Child?

IB, particularly the Diploma Programme, is rigorous and demanding. Your child must be prepared to spend significant time on his or her studies (including academic and service work).

Note that not every student in the IB program graduates with an IB Diploma. If your child successfully completes the IB Diploma Programme, he or she may be able to earn credit for first-year university courses.

Students in the IB Diploma Programme develop skills for community engagement through volunteer work.

Schools must pay the IB organization for membership, professional development for teachers, and administration and assessment of exams. These costs are normally passed on to the students and can be hundreds of dollars a year.

If you are interested in enrolling your child into an IB program, research the admission and application requirements. The demand frequently exceeds available spaces in both public and independent schools.

PRIMARY YEARS (AGES 3 TO 12)	• Encourages development of the whole child in both the class-room and the world outside of the school • Focuses on inquiry, real-world relevance, and transdisciplinary study	15 SCHOOLS IN BC
MIDDLE YEARS (AGES 11 TO 16)	• Focuses on development of global awareness and empathy, as well as creative, critical, and reflective thinking skills • Emphasizes service to the community • Encourages students to explore in depth a project of personal significance	17 SCHOOLS IN BC

DIPLOMA (AGES 16 TO 19)	• Encourages students to
	  ‣ develop deep knowledge
	  ‣ explore the nature of knowledge
	  ‣ complete projects that demonstrate creativity, action, and service
	Note: This is the program most people think of when they hear about the IB program.
		27 SCHOOLS IN BC

CAREER-RELATED (AGES 16 TO 19)	• Allows students to pursue a trade, apprenticeship, or technical education • Incorporates academic rigour and global awareness, encouraging students to think critically and ethically	0 SCHOOLS IN BC

International Baccalaureate programs

PART 3 PROGRAM AND SCHOOLING OPTIONS

ABORIGINAL EDUCATION PROGRAMS

The more than 66000 students in BC public schools who self-identify as Aboriginal are given opportunities to maintain their language, culture, and knowledge of history through the education system.[18] The BC Ministry of Education is working to ensure accurate and authentic integration of Aboriginal content, perspectives, and teaching in the school system. First Peoples Principles of Learning are reflected in the development of BC curriculum, including the principle that learning be "holistic, reflexive, reflective, experiential, and relational (focused on connectedness, on reciprocal relationships, and a sense of place)."[19] Respectful recognition of Aboriginal culture must take into account that culture and history are integral to student development and success.[20]

Schooling options that respect Aboriginal ways of knowing or that focus on holistic learning, including those shown on the opposite page, have emerged to help meet the needs of Aboriginal students and families.

Learning at Nusdeh Yoh Elementary School in Prince George is rooted in Aboriginal world views, culture, and language. Nusdeh Yoh means "House of the Future" in the Dakelh language.

Public school districts throughout the province have an obligation to provide programming and support for Aboriginal students. However, you may wish your child to benefit from a deeper level of Aboriginal learning and culture. If you live in an area served by a school offering an Aboriginal education program and you would like your child's understanding and experience to be enriched through Aboriginal learning, one of these programs might be the right choice.

ABORIGINAL EDUCATION PROGRAMS		
Program	**Description**	**Example**

Enhanced academic and cultural programming in public schools	• School districts work with Aboriginal communities to create Aboriginal Education Enhancement Agreements to support Aboriginal students.
	
	• School districts use provincial funding to
	  ‣ offer cultural programs
	  ‣ hire Aboriginal teachers and support workers
		School District No. 85 (Vancouver Island North) is located in the traditional Kwakwaka'wakw territory and offers
		
		• Kwak'wala language classes
		
		• a Role Model program in which Elders and other community members offer cultural teachings such as drum making, salmon smoking, and traditional dancing and singing[21]

Aboriginal schools of choice in the public system	• Some school districts with significant Aboriginal populations establish schools of choice to better serve the needs of Aboriginal students. • Any student in the district, regardless of ancestry, may attend the schools.	Nusdeh Yoh is a public school in School District No. 57 (Prince George) that offers • Kindergarten to Grade 7 education based on the BC curriculum • courses in Dakelh language, culture, and history • holistic teaching and learning, modelled after traditional First Nations ways of learning[22]

Schools administered by First Nations on Reserve Lands	• The Government of Canada and the Government of British Columbia recognize the right of First Nations people to educate their own children.
	
	• Many Aboriginal bands have established schools on reserve lands that are funded by Aboriginal Affairs and Northern Development Canada and may either be
	  ‣ band operated and not regulated through the BC education system, or
	  ‣ operated as independent schools subject to the *Independent Schools Act.*[23]
	
	• First Nations–administered schools are represented by the BC First Nations School Association.
		Eliza Archie Memorial School, administered by Canim Lake First Nation in Canim Lake, offers
		
		• Kindergarten to Grade 7 education based on the BC curriculum
		
		• Shuswap language and cultural activities
		
		• activities that promote healthy and active lifestyles through the Action Schools! BC program[24]

PART 3

PROGRAM AND SCHOOLING OPTIONS

ARTS PROGRAMS

All public schools incorporate the arts into the daily curriculum. Some have music specialists who teach music and choir, art programs such as painting and ceramics, or extracurricular art and dance opportunities. For many children, these options are enough, but if your child has particular interest or aptitude in the visual or performing arts, you may want to consider a school that has an arts program of choice. Some districts even have entire schools dedicated to the arts.

Is an Arts Program the Right Choice for Your Child?

For many parents, the decision to enroll their child in an arts program may seem like an easy one: *My child loves to draw and paint, so why not choose a school with an arts focus?*

Before enrolling your child in a dedicated arts program, it is important to consider that most children find some joy in the creative arts at an early age. Children who have a casual interest in the arts may find that they prefer a regular school program so that they are able to pursue other interests.

Similarly, some young children may show particular promise in one area of the arts but have little interest in other art forms. For example, a student with an aptitude for the visual arts may not have the personality or desire to engage in the performing arts, such as drama, music, or dance.

If you are considering an arts program for your child, it is important to understand the focus of the program, learn if instruction is focused on one or more areas of the arts, and determine if the program is the right fit for your child. An arts program may be appropriate for your child if he or she

- already engages in the arts either at home or through lessons or organized activities
- is comfortable with expressing him- or herself to others without a great deal of anxiety or nervousness
- shows a significant aptitude toward artistic endeavours

EXAMPLE

The Langley Fine Arts School (LFAS), a Grades 1–12 public school in School District No. 35 (Langley), is committed to fine arts education and provides "a comprehensive education for students, while focussing on the development of aesthetic intelligence through programmes in the Visual Arts, Literary Arts, Dance, Drama, and Music."[25] As well as teaching the regular BC curriculum, LFAS has a special focus on studying and appreciating world cultures, both ancient and modern.

In Grades 1 to 5, students are taught drama, dance, music, and visual arts. The arts are also heavily integrated into core academic studies. In the middle school, students focus on three of the four arts.

In Grades 8 to 12, students may start to focus their artistic passion. LFAS offers classes in dance, art, music, and drama, such as choreography, hip hop, orchestra, jazz, voice, painting, sculpture, and media arts. Writing, photography, and motion picture arts are also offered.

Arts programs offer a variety of visual and performing arts, including music.

SPORTS PROGRAMS

Sports and athletics can have an immeasurable impact on the lives of students. The discipline, healthy living, sense of community, and sense of belonging that come with being part of a sport or team brings lifetime benefits. Many schools and districts have created a variety of programs and partnerships to enhance student participation and engagement in athletics, as shown in the table on the opposite page.

Is a Sports Program the Right Choice for Your Child?

A sports program can provide significant added engagement for the right student. Before enrolling your child in one of these programs, consider the following factors:

Brentwood College is renowned for its rowing program. It hosts the annual Brentwood International Rowing Regatta, a competition that attracts teams from all over the world.

- Most sports programs focus on only one sport, so it is important to ensure that your child is sufficiently interested in the sport to remain committed throughout the program.
- Many sports programs require some level of experience before a student will be considered and are not designed for novices in the sport of focus.
- A sports program may be the right choice for your child if he or she
  ‣ is already playing a sport at a competitive level and would benefit from additional conditioning
  ‣ has been playing a sport and would like to further develop his or her skills and abilities
  ‣ demonstrates self-motivation and commitment

SPORT PROGRAMS		
Program	**Description**	**Example**

Sports Academy	• Offers enhanced athletic opportunities
	
	• May operate in conjunction with universities, sport associations, and professional or minor league teams
		• The Snowsports Academy in School District No. 22 (Vernon) allows students in Grades 8 to 12 to
		  ‣ participate in their choice of alpine, freestyle, or Nordic skiing
		  ‣ earn at least 2 credits toward graduation
		  ‣ receive expert instruction and dryland training, and spend two days on the hill every week during ski season
		• Students receive academic support to help make up for missed classroom time and may supplement their school work with distributed learning classes.[26]

Elite Athlete Program	• Accommodates students who frequently miss school for high-level practices and competitions • Allows students to engage in sports while completing school curriculum requirements	• The Elite Performers in Coquitlam (EPIC) program in School District No. 43 (Coquitlam) is open to secondary school students who are top performers in athletics, theatre, music, dance, or modelling (based on set criteria). • Students are assigned an advisor-counsellor to help liaise between the school, parents, coaches, and instructors. • Students are given flexibility in coursework, stress management support, an individualized learning schedule, credits toward graduation through their sport or discipline, and the opportunity to take distributed learning classes.[27]
Magnet School	• Embraces a particular sport so successfully that the school earns a reputation of excellence in the sport	• Brentwood College School, an independent school on Vancouver Island, is a magnet school in rowing. • Alumni include 22 Olympic athletes. • Over 175 graduates have gone on to row at universities, and graduates have earned a combined total of more than $9 million in post-secondary scholarships. • Brentwood rowers have competed in world championships at the junior and senior levels for multiple countries.[28]
Franchise School	• Operates in partnership with an athletic team	• BC's six Western Hockey League (WHL) hockey teams have franchise schools attended by the school-aged players. For example, players from the Prince George Cougars attend College Heights Secondary School in School District No. 57 (Prince George). • Each team has an education advisor who monitors student performance, works with school staff, and provides assistance to student athletes.[29]

MONTESSORI AND REGGIO EMILIA PROGRAMS

Montessori and Reggio Emilia are two philosophies of and approaches to early childhood education. They are offered in some BC elementary schools and preschools, both public and independent.

Montessori: educational philosophy developed by Italian physician and educator Maria Montessori

Reggio Emilia: educational philosophy developed by Italian educator Loris Malaguzzi

MONTESSORI AND REGGIO EMILIA PROGRAMS		
Program	**Description**	**Example**
Montessori	• Values individual student choice, and balances whole class and individual learning • Encourages students to learn at their own pace and pursue their own interests • Teaches values of individual learning, respecting others, citizenship, and experiential education (or learning through doing) • Taught by teachers certified in the Montessori Method	• School District No. 38 (Richmond) offers the Montessori program at three elementary schools: Garden City, McKinney, and Steves. • Often, students are organized into "family groups" of students from two or three grades. • Ideally, children will remain with the same teacher for three years to experience being the youngest and oldest student in the classroom.[30]
Reggio Emilia	• Is similar to Montessori but is a less formal model (no formal accreditation or teacher certification) • Encourages students to think critically, explore, and question • Focuses on project-based learning and places a heavy influence on the arts, problem solving, and conflict resolution	• Meadowbrook Elementary in School District No. 43 (Coquitlam) is a Reggio Emilia–influenced public school. • The entire school—from Kindergarten to Grade 5—follows the philosophy's guiding principles. • It uses the Reggio Emilia approach to developing student engagement, self-regulation, creativity, and co-operation.[31]

Is a Montessori or Reggio Emilia Program the Right Choice for Your Child?

The Montessori philosophy emphasizes students' individual choice in their learning. While pillars of the philosophy, including citizenship and experiential learning, are implemented in the regular school system, they are stated more explicitly in Montessori. Children in the program are encouraged to do hands-on work and exercise choice in what they are learning. If these values are important to you, you may wish to enroll your child in a Montessori program.

The Reggio Emilia approach incorporates many opportunities for group work and project-based learning, with an emphasis on self-regulation. Children learn about how to monitor and control their emotions. Teachers focus less on giving direction and more on encouraging students to explore their environments. If your child is a social learner and can work with little adult direction, a Reggio Emilia classroom may be appropriate.

Montessori classrooms are designed to foster student independence and hands-on learning. Learning materials are stored within easy reach and work spaces encourage group work.

66 *Montessori educational practice helps children develop creativity, problem solving, critical thinking and time-management skills, [and] care of the environment and each other, and prepares them to contribute to society and to become fulfilled persons.* 99

—The International Montessori Index[32]

CHALLENGE PROGRAMS

challenge program:
a program for
elementary students
that challenges
them beyond the
requirements of the
regular curriculum

Challenge is an elementary program in which students remain enrolled at their regular school but engage in an enriched program of study about one day a week. Students from across the district meet at one school to participate in the program.

Depending on the age of the students and the interests and skill sets of the teachers, these programs may offer such diverse learning as building robots or structures, photography, hands-on science, or other creative options.

Some districts also have challenge programs for "twice exceptional" students: children who have both an identified learning disability and giftedness.

Is a Challenge Program the Right Choice for Your Child?

Schools nominate children for the challenge program, with nominations evaluated at the district level. Normally, far more students are nominated than there are available spaces.

Nominated children are identified by their teacher as being bright (but not necessarily gifted), or as having a particular aptitude that makes them well suited for the program. You may also ask your child's teacher or principal to consider your child for the program. In the nomination process, you and your child's teacher may be required to complete paperwork describing your child's abilities, learning style, and temperament. If your child is selected for the program, expect to arrange transportation to the school where the program takes place.

EXAMPLE

School District No. 62 (Sooke) offers a program of enriching, "mind-extending" activities and interactions with guest speakers on a variety of topics.[33] Students from various elementary schools travel on regular mornings to Colwood Elementary for this program.

MULTI-AGE CLUSTER CLASSES

The multi-age cluster class (MACC) program is a district program for gifted elementary learners. Students are challenged to develop their critical thinking skills through interdisciplinary study.

Students within the program show great curiosity but often have difficulty socializing in classroom situations. MACC classes address students' difficulties in social situations by focusing on tasks and project work. Teachers often give little direction so that students use their creativity to complete assignments. The curriculum tends to emphasize exploration and innovation, as opposed to content.

Is a MACC Program the Right Choice for Your Child?

Entrance into a MACC program is through a comprehensive screening and application process that involves examination of students' marks, intelligence and aptitude testing, and student interviews. The ideal candidates for the MACC program are not always students who just work hard and do well in school, but rather have the ability to think abstractly.

MACC is a full-time program. If your child is accepted to the program, he or she may be required to change schools and you are responsible for your child's transportation.

multi-age cluster class (MACC) program: a program for highly gifted elementary students that provides academic challenge, as well as social-emotional support

PART 3

PROGRAM AND SCHOOLING OPTIONS

EXAMPLE

School District No. 39 (Vancouver) states that

Grade 4–7 students will be considered for the [MACC] class based on skill development, cognitive abilities, intellectual interests, creativity, and emotional maturity. Minimum criteria typically include

- reading and mathematic skills two or more grades above grade level

- demonstrated ability to focus on tasks, enjoyment of complexity and marked motivation to learn quickly and to learn advanced level material[34]

VOCATIONAL PROGRAMS

vocational program: a school program that allows secondary students to specialize in a trade such as carpentry, cooking, or metal fabrication

British Columbia has a strong need for skilled tradespeople. Vocational programs in the province's secondary schools lead students toward rewarding careers in any number of trades. Today's vocational programs are competitive and desirable options that provide world-class training and can take your child to a career where high wages are the industry standard.

Vocational and apprenticeship programs include those listed on the following page.

Is a Vocational Program the Right Choice for Your Child?

There was a time when students were identified as "academic" and destined for university or "non-academic" and placed into workplace training. Many parents preferred the academic programs because they believed that a university education would provide the best career options for their children. Those days are over! If your child has an aptitude for a trade—from automotive service to cooking, hairstyling, or welding, among many others—and is a "hands-on" learner, then a vocational program might be an excellent choice.

Students who successfully complete the Secondary School Apprenticeship may qualify for a $1000 scholarship from the provincial government.[35]

VOCATIONAL AND APPRENTICESHIP PROGRAMS		
Program	**Description**	**Example**
Accelerated Credit Enrollment in Industry Training (ACE IT)	• Is often combined with the Secondary School Apprenticeship program, forming the in-class component of vocational training • Allows students in Grades 11 and 12 to earn credit toward graduation and credit toward certification in the Industry Training Authority (ITA) program • Offers more than 50 different trades, including automotive painting, cabinetmaking, cooking, and hairdressing	• The Career and Technical Centre (CTC) is a partnership between School District No. 57 (Prince George) and the College of New Caledonia. • In Grades 11 and 12, students spend two semesters in secondary school and two semesters at the college, earning both college and secondary school credit. • Program options include carpentry, dental assisting, plumbing, and welding.[36]
Secondary School Apprenticeship (SSA)	• Allows students to work as paid apprentices in the industry while completing secondary school • Can be completed concurrently with the ACE IT program • Open to students aged 15 years or older in Grades 11 and 12	
School to Work	• Allows students under 20 years of age who have not completed all their graduation credits to finish secondary school, earn post-secondary credits, and receive formal vocational training • Provides students with job-ready skills and certification	• School District No. 41 (Burnaby) offers a comprehensive School to Work program as part of its Community and Continuing Education department.[37]
Co-operative Program	• Some programs are designed to provide students with learning and/or behavioural challenges with hands-on work experience. • Others are for students who are looking for work experience in an industry that may not have an apprenticeship or ACE IT component.	• Several schools in School District No. 39 (Vancouver) offer Life Skills programs for students with autism, behavioural challenges, and/or cognitive disabilities. • The programs provide work experience and life skills training to prepare students for the transition out of school.[38]

OTHER PROGRAMS OF CHOICE

In addition to the schools and programs listed in this section, there are several other programs of choice available to students in British Columbia.

Traditional Schools

traditional school: a school that emphasizes traditional instructional models

Traditional schools embrace a "back to basics" approach that may include such elements as

- less co-operative learning and more teacher-directed instruction
- uniforms
- formal structures such as desks in rows
- regular homework
- strict behavioural codes

EXAMPLE

The following districts operate traditional schools:

- School District No. 34 (Abbotsford) has three traditional elementary schools, one traditional middle school, and one traditional secondary school.

- School District No. 36 (Surrey) offers traditional Kindergarten to Grade 7 education at Cloverdale Traditional, McLeod Road Traditional, and Surrey Traditional.

- School District No. 33 (Chilliwack) offers a traditional program at McCammon Traditional Elementary.

Year-Round or Balanced-Calendar Schools

balanced-calendar school: a school that operates on a year-round calendar, with classes typically in session for three months, followed by a one-month break

A small number of BC public schools operate year-round, or as balanced-calendar schools. These schools shift the vacation times in the school year in order to provide a more even balance of learning time to vacation time. While schools on the traditional calendar are closed for vacation in July and August, as well as during winter and spring breaks, balanced-calendar schools typically are in session year-round with one-month vacations in December, April, and August.

This system is based on the belief that students lose less of their acquired skills and knowledge with shorter breaks spaced evenly throughout the school year. Balanced-calendar schools have been the subject of much research and debate in school jurisdictions throughout North America. While some research claims educational benefits to the system, other research indicates little significant difference in learning or achievement—positive or negative—between the two systems.[39]

EXAMPLE

The following elementary schools operate on a balanced calendar:

- Douglas Park Community School in School District No. 35 (Langley)

- Garden City Elementary in School District No. 38 (Richmond)

- Kanaka Creek Elementary in School District No. 42 (Maple Ridge–Pitt Meadows)

Outdoor/Experiential Education Programs

Outdoor/experiential education programs vary from school to school. The focus of some programs is to provide opportunities for students to participate in activities such as mountaineering, camping, sailing, and kayaking. Other programs place more focus on learning about the natural environment, sustainability, and ways people affect the environment (and vice versa), through activities such as salmon habitat enhancement and other stewardship programs.

outdoor/ experiential education program: a program that emphasizes outdoor learning

Maple Ridge Environmental School in School District No. 42 (Maple Ridge–Pitt Meadows) offers Kindergarten to Grade 7 education that focuses on reconnecting the natural and human worlds.

EXAMPLE

The following outdoor/experiential education programs are among many offered throughout the province:

- School District No. 39 (Vancouver): TREK program at Prince of Wales Secondary School

- School District No. 42 (Maple Ridge–Pitt Meadows): Maple Ridge Environmental School

- School District No. 47 (Powell River): Coast Mountain Academy

- School District No. 78 (Fraser-Cascade): Fraser-Cascade Mountain School

- School District No. 84 (Vancouver Island West): Nootka Sound Outdoor Program

Inquiry and Self-Directed Programs

Some districts offer students the opportunity to direct their own program of study. These programs attract students who enjoy independent learning, technology, and projects.

In these programs, the regular classroom structure is either non-existent or limited, with teachers serving as learning facilitators while students work at their own pace and on their own material. Some schools have self-directed programs within a regular school environment, while others adopt the self-directed model school-wide.

EXAMPLE

Schools offering school-wide self-directed programs in British Columbia include

- Thomas Haney Secondary School in School District No. 42 (Maple Ridge–Pitt Meadows)

- Frances Kelsey Secondary School in School District No. 79 (Cowichan Valley)

University Highlands Elementary School in School District No. 41 (Burnaby) offers the Learning in Depth program, based on the work of Kieran Egan.[40] Students study and become experts in a topic they continue to develop throughout their entire school career, in addition to the regular, prescribed curriculum.

Independent Directed Studies

Within the secondary Graduation Program, the Ministry of Education has created an Independent Directed Studies (IDS) policy, which "enables students to initiate their own area of learning."[41] That is, a student may design his or her own course around one or more Prescribed Learning Outcomes of an existing course. The ministry states: "This policy is not a student entitlement but an enabling policy intended to encourage schools to allow students to pursue further studies of interest."[42] For example, a student with an interest in biology may choose to do an in-depth, inquiry-based study of one learning outcome, or a broader study of a number of learning outcomes from Biology 11 or 12, and elect to pursue inquiry around the learning outcome of DNA Replication or the Human Circulatory System.

Independent Directed Studies may be right for students who are motivated, inquisitive, and able to work with little direction or supervision.

IDS courses are designed to provide flexibility for students to study, in depth, an area of their own interest or passion. IDS courses can be 1 to 4 credits, depending primarily on the depth of the course inquiry and the length of time students commit to the study. A 4-credit course is considered to be approximately 90 hours of study.

Most school districts identify specific criteria for designing an IDS course. A teacher is responsible for evaluating whether the student has met the learning outcomes. Often students also have a mentor who can provide information or assistance to the student during his or her study. For example, a biology student may make contact with a researcher at the local college or university and meet with that researcher as part of the study. Some districts (typically larger ones, where there are many students taking an IDS course) may have a teacher who manages or supervises all the IDS students in a given school or region.

PART 4

Learning Support and Behaviour Interventions

KEY QUESTIONS

- What happens if you, or staff at your child's school, believe your child might benefit from additional support?

- What additional support is available, and how will this look in your child's classroom?

- What support is available to students who are learning English?

- What should you do if you suspect your child is being bullied?

- What interventions or supports might be implemented if students have behaviour issues?

WOULD YOUR CHILD BENEFIT FROM ADDITIONAL LEARNING SUPPORT?

Throughout your child's K–12 school years, teachers will share with you their observations about your child's learning and behaviour. What happens if a teacher suggests that your child needs additional support?

Identifying the Issue

Teachers may observe that your child has difficulty with language processing, behaviour, or any number of issues that affect learning. They may also identify if your child varies from age-level expectations. They are *never* tasked with diagnosis of disorders, but will suggest that your child needs further diagnosis. The school will follow established procedures to determine how best to meet your child's needs:

- You may be asked to complete a questionnaire to help professionals identify potential challenges.
- Your child may be referred for comprehensive psychometric testing, which is completed by a school psychologist.
- Your child may be assessed through the public health system.

The time required to diagnose a disorder—from when you first suspect your child may have special needs to a diagnosis—will depend on the severity of the condition. The health-care system and the school system use a triage process, in which the most serious issues are dealt with first and other issues are dealt with afterwards. Depending on the school and the needs of its population, it may be necessary to continually reprioritize the list of children who need to be tested. The diagnostic process can be completed in as little as three months or as long as two years.

You may choose to pay privately for assessment, which can result in a shorter waiting period. It is essential that, if you decide to pay for private assessment services, you fully disclose the results to the school. This is the only way a school can implement all potential supports and best meet the needs of your child.

What Supports Are Available?

If your child has been diagnosed with **special needs**, you may hear the term **designation**: this refers to formal identification of a student's needs based on categories established by the Ministry of Education. Designations are categorized by the amount of support a student requires and are differentiated by the letters A to H. The Ministry of Education provides the school with funding to support students with designations, as shown in the following table.

SPECIAL NEEDS DESIGNATIONS AND FUNDING (2014/2015)[1]	
Description of Designation	**Funding**
Level 1 • Physically dependent (A) • Deafblind (B)	$36 600
Level 2 • Moderate to profound intellectual disability (C) • Physical disability or chronic health impairment (D) • Visual impairment (E) • Deaf or hard of hearing (F) • Autism spectrum disorder (G)	$18 300
Level 3 • Intensive behaviour interventions or serious mental illness (H)	$9200

Your child is eligible for only one category of funding, even if he or she has multiple designations. For example, a student who is deaf and has serious behaviour issues (designations F and H) qualifies only for Level 2 funding.

Funds allocated for a child with special needs help pay for district special needs resources, rather than going directly to the designated child. For example, the funding designated for a child with autism spectrum disorder (Level 2) is $18 300 plus the base funding of $6900, for a total of $25 200. This $25 200 covers learning assistance, as well as classroom resources and a portion of the salaries of school staff.

special needs, student with: a student who has an intellectual, physical, sensory, emotional, or behavioural disability; learning disability; or exceptional gifts or talents

designation: an identification of a student's special needs, as recognized by the BC Ministry of Education

PART 4

LEARNING SUPPORT AND BEHAVIOUR INTERVENTIONS

> *All students should have equitable access to learning, opportunities for achievement, and the pursuit of excellence in all aspects of their educational programs.*
>
> —BC Ministry of Education, 2013[2]

Most schools cannot afford to provide individualized care on a full-time basis for any single student. They meet the needs of each child within the constraints of the funding system. The amount of support required for students within each of the designation levels also varies. For example, within the H designation, a child who has severe mental illness such as psychosis likely requires more resources than a child with anxiety. If your child has been designated with special needs, the school administrators must determine how much support your child receives based on the funding and resources available.

How Will Your Child's Needs Be Met in the Classroom?

If your child has special learning needs, you will be invited to a consultation meeting with school staff, applicable school district staff, and other professionals. Depending on the nature of his or her designation, your child may also be invited. The following issues are discussed during the meeting:

- the nature of your child's learning challenges
- the goals he or she will work toward
- the learning strategies and support structures recommended
- the specific roles of the support team

Individual Education Plan (IEP): a plan based on a student's specific learning needs to help him or her be successful at school

adaptations: alternative teaching and assessment strategies that accommodate the learning needs of a student with special needs

modifications: individualized learning goals that reflect a student's educational needs

An **Individual Education Plan (IEP)** is produced as a result of this meeting. The IEP outlines any accommodations that need to be made to teaching and assessment strategies or learning goals to meet your child's needs. Accommodations can include **adaptations** and/or **modifications**. Note that a student at the secondary level whose IEP includes modifications earns credits toward a BC School Completion Certificate (Evergreen Certificate) rather than a BC Certificate of Graduation (Dogwood Diploma).

Your child's IEP must be approved by you, your child's teacher, and the principal. A follow-up meeting is held later in the school year to review your child's progress and make changes to the IEP as required.

Education assistants work under the direction of the teacher and principal to facilitate the inclusion of students with special needs in classroom.

Your child may work with any of the following specialized staff:

- **Learning Support (or Resource) Teacher:** a person specially trained to work with students with learning disabilities
- **Education Assistant (EA):** a support worker for students with special needs, such as toileting, or behavioural problems
- **Speech–Language Pathologist (SLP):** a professional who works with people with communication difficulties, such as speech impediments
- **Psychologist:** a professional who completes complex assessments to identify learning disabilities
- **Hearing and Vision Teachers:** specially trained teachers who work with students with hearing and vision disabilities

EXAMPLE

The complexity of the IEP depends on the specific learning needs of the student. The following examples illustrate the wide variability in the support students may require within each designation:

- Jasminder is a Grade 4 student with a mild form of autism (G designation). She is academically capable, but struggles with responding verbally to questions and social interactions. She needs support to play with friends and answer questions.

- Tony is a Grade 4 student with a severe form of autism (G designation). He is non-verbal, aggressive, and requires one-on-one special support from an education assistant.

PART 4

LEARNING SUPPORT AND BEHAVIOUR INTERVENTIONS

Special Needs Programs

Some students have learning or behavioural challenges that cannot be adequately addressed in the regular classroom, and many districts have created alternative elementary programs to meet these students' needs. Because these programs offer a more focused approach to dealing with special needs, as well as a higher adult-to-student ratio, students often achieve more success than they would in the mainstream school system. In some cases, the intervention gives children the support they need to transition back to the regular school.

Some programs are self-contained, small, multi-age classes with little interaction with the main body of the school. In other programs, students are enrolled in a regular class but receive support from a counsellor, youth worker, and/or education assistant. They may also receive support from agencies such as the health authority and the Ministry for Children and Family Development.

It is important to stress that a special needs designation doesn't mean that your child is "bad." Rather, it is recognition that your child requires additional support to manage his or her special needs. There can be many different reasons for the special needs, including medical or mental health conditions. Your child cannot be placed in such a program without your consent, but these special programs are designed to better meet your child's learning needs. Here are some key questions you should ask:

- To what degree are students in the program integrated into the life of the school?
- What supports are offered to my child?
- Does the school district provide transportation to the program?
- Who makes the decision that my child is ready (or not ready) to return to the neighbourhood school?
- How frequently will the school provide me with updates on my child's progress?

DOES YOUR CHILD NEED ENGLISH LANGUAGE SUPPORT?

You may see the acronyms ELL and ESL in discussions of English language support in the school system. ESL (English as a Second Language) is now referred to as ELL (English Language Learner).

Even if your child was born in Canada, the school may designate your child as ELL if the language spoken at home is not English. Identifying a student as ELL makes the school eligible for additional funding from the Ministry of Education, which was $1340 per student for the 2014/2015 school year.[3] A child retains ELL status for five years after beginning school.

English Language Learners receive an **Annual Instructional Plan (AIP)** that identifies

- goals for the child's English language learning
- materials and adaptations that will enhance learning
- assessments to measure progress

Annual Instructional Plan (AIP): a learning plan for an English Language Learner

The school's learning assistance department often provides the additional support needed by English Language Learners. If you are told that your child will be receiving learning assistance, it is recommended that you arrange to meet with school staff to discuss your child's learning.

The amount of English language support also varies from grade to grade and from student to student. Schools provide support such as small group learning, specific ELL classes, and in-class help. ELL support also varies by course subject. A Grade 9 student with ELL designation may not be in English 9 but in a specific ELL class. That same student, however, may have sufficient English language proficiency to be in a regular math class. It is good practice to provide each learner with the appropriate level of instruction in the best environment possible.

An important component of students' English language learning is language practice with their peers. This can be a challenge in areas with homogeneous ethnic populations, such as Surrey, where approximately 40 per cent of the school population is Punjabi. English language acquisition can be slowed when students do not use English in their interactions with other students.

PART 4

LEARNING SUPPORT AND BEHAVIOUR INTERVENTIONS

LEARNING SUPPORT AND BEHAVIOUR INTERVENTIONS

The following are answers to some frequently asked questions about ELL:

- **Why didn't I know my child was receiving ELL learning assistance until I received the report card?**

  If your child has been receiving ELL learning assistance and you didn't know it, then you should have a conversation with the principal immediately. Schools are required to inform parents that their children have been designated as ELL.

- **Why does my child have to receive ELL designation?**

  The designation enables the school to provide students with the support they need to become proficient in English. Your child's level of English proficiency is a key factor in determining whether he or she needs extra assistance.

- **Why does my child have to leave the classroom for learning assistance?**

  This depends on the specific needs of your child. Some students receive intensive support because of a significant challenge. For example, some instructional strategies require students to receive one-on-one support. Instead of enrolling in an elective course, secondary students may have a specific block where they work with a learning support teacher to get personalized help.

Frequent practice is an important factor in language learning. You can support children's language learning by encouraging them to use English outside the classroom.

WHAT CAN YOU DO IF YOUR CHILD IS BEING BULLIED?

It sometimes seems that not a day goes by without a student or parent (on behalf of the student) alleging that bullying has occurred. When dealing with school staff about such a situation, it is often helpful to describe the incident instead of labelling it.

It is important to understand the difference between conflict and bullying. The BC Ministry of Education explains the distinction as follows:

- **Conflict** is a disagreement between peers who have equal power in the relationship. It is often an inevitable part of group interactions.
- **Bullying** is an ongoing pattern of unwelcome behaviour that tends to involve an imbalance of power in the relationship, and/or intent to harm or humiliate.[4]

Experts identify four types of bullying:

- physical, which includes hitting, kicking, and damaging property
- verbal, which includes name-calling, teasing, and verbal abuse
- social-emotional, which includes actions designed to cause humiliation (for example, spreading rumours)
- cyber, which includes taunting through social media[5]

Bullying situations often begin as cyberbullying and continue at school in the form of physical, verbal, or social-emotional bullying. Children tend to be more brazen on the Internet, and may be more likely to engage in negative interactions than they would in face-to-face situations.

A consequence that is sometimes overlooked when speaking about bullying is the effect the term may have on the victim. Encourage your child to talk to you so that, together, you can find tangible solutions. This may mean getting the school involved or even going to the police, but it is important to identify solutions to empower your child, rather than simply identifying an incident as bullying.

> " *Some kids may use bullying as a way to enhance their social power and protect their prestige with their peers. Some kids actually use bullying to deflect taunting and aggression that is directed toward them—a form of self protection.* "
>
> —BC Ministry of Education[6]

PART 4

LEARNING SUPPORT AND BEHAVIOUR INTERVENTIONS

It is often believed that schools have a "zero-tolerance policy" for bullying. For the most part, this notion is inaccurate. In their combined 50 years of school leadership experience, the authors of this book have found that few situations call for "zero tolerance." Most schools have a zero-tolerance policy for *inaction* in cases of bullying, but they work with the school population to solve problems that arise. All those involved in a situation of alleged bullying will have different perspectives, and school staff must consider all sides of the situation. When discussing an incident with school staff, try to describe the incident as objectively as possible.

All schools are required by the *School Act* to have a code of conduct. It is a good idea to familiarize yourself with the code of conduct at your child's school, particularly if you need to discuss possible behavioural issues with the school.

One of the best resources for information on bullying is the BC Ministry of Education's ERASE (Expect Respect, and a Safe Education) Bullying website, which provides a wide variety of resources, from a reporting tool to strategies for how to deal with specific situations.

c. Retaliation against individuals who have reported breaches of our Code of Conduct;
d. Watching, filming or encouraging bullying or fighting;
e. Illegal acts such as possession, use, or distribution of any restricted, unsafe, or illegal materials/substances;
f. Possession or use of any item that
g. Attempted theft, theft and/or dam
h. Abusive and profane language.

Consequences:
Whenever possible, incidents will be
mediation and restitution. School res
consistent and fair; responses and are fra
philosophy. We will respect the individua
each situation according to the student's
As students mature there is an expectation
characteristics of increased personal resp

Notification:
Minor infractions will be worked ou
informed. For major infractions, p
informed by school officials. This
letter mailed home, and/or a mee
additional agencies such as the p
will be informed.

BC Human Rights Code
All participants in school activities,
accordance with the BC Human R
fairness. No person shall discri
publication, or service.

Merritt Secondary School
Code of Conduct
2014/2015

Purpose:
The purpose of the Code of Conduct is to support our Vision/Mission Statement:

"To inspire and empower one another to lead purposeful lives. We will passionately and respectfully engage one another to recognize and reach our individual potential."

Expectations:
These expectations are for all members of our school community while in attendance at school, while travelling to and from school, and while attending any school function at any location.

I. **Examples of Exemplary Conduct include the following:**
   a. Be truthful and trustworthy;
   b. Demonstrate respect for self, others, and the school;
   c. Assist in making the school a safe and respectful facility;
   d. Inform staff of incidents of bullying, harassment, intimidation or violence and discourage such acts;
   e. Participate in acts that bring credit to the school;
   f. Be a positive role model;
   g. Recognize our cultural diversity and act in a manner that ensures safety for all cultures in our school;
   h. Attend all classes on time, prepared to work.

II. **Examples of Unacceptable Conduct include these behaviours:**

UNDERSTANDING INTERVENTIONS OR SUPPORTS FOR BEHAVIOUR ISSUES

At some point in your child's schooling, you may be called into the classroom, counsellor's room, or principal's office to discuss something that your child has done. You may also hear from your child about how he or she has been wronged in various situations.

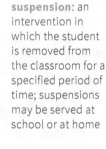

Keep in mind that educators hope that parents will help to uphold the school's code of conduct. Behavioural expectations are clearer for students when parents, teachers, and administrators are all supportive of school policies.

The school's code of conduct may outline forms of unacceptable conduct and describe possible consequences:

- Minor incidents may result in informal interventions such as detentions or in-school **suspension**. Generally, an informal intervention may be appealed to the principal.

- More serious incidents may result in formal intervention, including at-home suspension or a review of a child's placement within the school. Formal intervention is documented in the student's permanent school record.

  If your child is suspended and sent home, he or she is expected to complete school work. You are expected to accompany your child back to the school after the suspension is completed for a meeting with school administrators. Following a suspension, in-school counselling is often recommended.

- If a situation involves criminal code offences such as uttering threats or harassment, the school will involve the School Liaison Officer, a member of the local police force.

- Students with Individual Education Plans (IEPs) may face different forms of intervention, tailored to their needs.

Note that independent schools may have different forms of intervention from those described here.

suspension: an intervention in which the student is removed from the classroom for a specified period of time; suspensions may be served at school or at home

Students should familiarize themselves with the code of conduct to understand what behaviour is and is not acceptable at school.

PART 5

Assessment and Evaluation

KEY QUESTIONS

- What is the difference between assessment and evaluation?

- Why is assessment important?

- How is your child's learning assessed and evaluated?

- What information is provided on report cards? Against what performance standards is your child evaluated?

- How can you make the most of parent–teacher interviews?

THE DIFFERENCE BETWEEN ASSESSMENT AND EVALUATION

assessment: an ongoing process that helps teachers and students understand how well students are learning; is not graded

evaluation: a judgment on the performance of the student at the end of a unit of study; based on learning outcomes; includes marks/grades

No aspect of school generates more questions and creates more anxiety for both parents and students than assessment and evaluation. There is also no other educational topic that has so much confusing language and jargon. *Formative, summative, assessment for learning, assessment as learning, assessment of learning, letter grade/mark/percentage, performance standard, PLO (Prescribed Learning Outcome)*—the list goes on and on. Parents are often frustrated and confused when all they want to know is: *How is my child doing?*

Simply stated, assessment is an ongoing, interactive process that helps teachers (and students) understand how well students are learning so that adjustments can be made to teaching for the students' benefit. Assessment is *not* graded. Evaluation *is* graded, and occurs at the end of a unit of study to determine what students have learned.

ASSESSMENT IS	EVALUATION IS
• ongoing, occurring throughout a unit of study	• often a one-time event, occurring at the end of a unit of study
• formative, focusing on improving learning	• summative, focusing on a final outcome or result
• an interactive process between teacher and learner, often provided through descriptive feedback	• not interactive, but rather a judgment on the performance of the student
• used by teachers to adjust instruction	• an assessment of the student's learning with respect to the performance standards or Prescribed Learning Outcomes of the course
• a measure of what students know or don't know (also called *assessment* **for** *learning*)	
• focused on the learning process, rather than grades	• focused on the product and grades
• a process that provides students with an understanding of their own learning, such as through peer- or self-assessment (also called *assessment* **as** *learning*)	• also called *assessment* **of** *learning*

ASSESSMENT

Formative assessment practices are also called *assessment for learning* and *assessment as learning*. Research indicates that sound, effective assessment *for* learning practices, such as feedback, have one of the greatest effects on increasing student learning and engagement. Consistently, assessment *for* learning practices

- lead to significant gains in student achievement
- allow struggling learners to make the greatest gains
- are powerfully linked to student motivation
- are the next best thing to one-on-one tutoring
- lead to higher grades when evaluation takes place[1]

The following are some examples of what assessment might look like in the classroom:

- A Grade 9 math teacher gives her class a Grade 8 math pre-test at the start of the semester. The test is not graded but is used to determine what her students know or don't know and to guide instruction.
- A Grade 11 English teacher provides a student with feedback on an essay. He tells the student what she did well and why, what she needs to improve and why, and what she needs to do to earn maximum grades on the assignment.
- A Grade 4 teacher gives her class an anonymous survey on a project they completed, asking students what they did well, what they could improve, and what she could have done to help support their learning.
- Students are asked to assess their classmates' presentations using a rubric.

> **"** Feedback has been shown to improve learning when it gives each pupil specific guidance on strengths and weaknesses, preferably without any overall marks. **"**
>
> —Black & Wiliam, 2010[2]

A rubric is a chart that provides criteria at different levels of achievement.

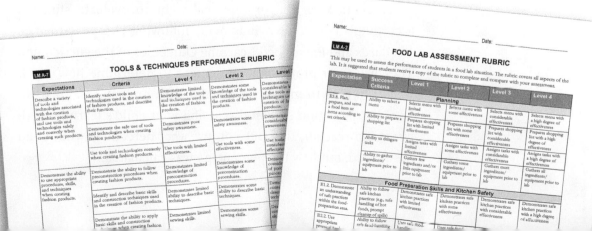

EVALUATION

Summative evaluation practices are also called *assessment of learning*. Evaluation is formal reporting of student learning, typically provided in the form of number ($\frac{8}{10}$ or 80 per cent) or letter (A, B, C+) grades, and is what many parents are most familiar with from their own schooling. It reveals where a student's learning is in relation to the performance standards or Prescribed Learning Outcomes of a particular course as set out in the curriculum.

The following are some examples of what evaluation might look like in the classroom:

- A teacher collects completed homework and assigns a grade.
- A teacher collects a completed in-class assignment or project and assigns a grade.
- Students write a test or exam in a course and the mark is applied to the final grade.

Teachers use a variety of formal and informal procedures to report student progress to students and parents. The *School Act* requires student progress to be reported at least five times throughout each school year, of which three must be formal written reports. The remaining reports may include informal written reports, telephone calls, or parent–teacher interviews.

Understanding Grade Calculation

Parents tend to want to see letter grades and percentages when discussing their children's learning. They often believe that they are more objective than descriptive feedback. It is important to realize, however, that even number or letter grades can produce very different results for a student, depending on how the teacher uses them.

Teachers have the professional right to evaluate students according to their own judgment, following the performance standards and Prescribed Learning Outcomes of the curriculum. They use their professional judgment to determine how much weight to give to individual assignments, projects, and tests in a grade calculation. When discussing your child's learning with his or her teacher, find out not just *what* percentage your child has earned, but *how* the percentage was calculated.

Primary Level Report Cards

At the primary level (Kindergarten to Grade 3), the aspect of evaluation that gives some parents the most concern is that primary students do not receive letter grades. The rationale for this policy is that, developmentally, evaluating younger students against a fixed point such as a letter grade or percentage is not appropriate.

EXAMPLE

Primary report cards evaluate student learning with respect to performance standards, such as these for Grade 2 Reading Literature:[3]

Not Yet Within Expectations	Meets Expectations (Minimal Level)	Fully Meets Expectations	Exceeds Expectations
The student needs one-to-one support to read short, simple stories and to attempt comprehension activities.	The student reads a variety of short, simple stories with understanding if given some support. Work is partially accurate.	The student reads a variety of short, simple stories independently and with understanding. Work is generally accurate.	The student reads an increasing variety of simple stories independently and with understanding. Work is clear, accurate, and complete.

Primary report cards across the province all contain similar elements, including

- a brief description of what students are learning
- for each area of study, a description of what the student can do in relation to the performance standards, where he or she needs additional support, and how the parent can support the student at home
- a description of the student's social-emotional abilities, behaviour, and ability to solve problems, work with others, and so on
- an indication of whether the student is meeting the Daily Physical Activity (DPA) requirements
- an indication of whether the student has an Individual Education Plan (IEP) (see page 84)
- an indication of whether the student has an Annual Instructional Plan (AIP) (see page 87)
- information on the student's attendance record

Daily Physical Activity (DPA) requirements: the minimum amount (30 minutes) of physical activity a student must do during the school day, as specified by the BC Ministry of Education

ASSESSMENT AND EVALUATION

PART 5

Intermediate and Secondary Level Report Cards

At the intermediate level (Grades 4 to 7), students receive letter grades as indicators of their achievement for each subject. Intermediate teachers also include written comments with specific information about the student's progress.

At the secondary level (Grades 8 to 12), students receive letter grades and short written comments. Because secondary teachers may have between 120 and 210 students to evaluate, comments tend to be standard computerized notes such as "needs to hand work in on time" or "demonstrates a good understanding of...." Percentages are not mandated until students reach Grade 10.

The following table shows the letter grades and percentages used for report cards in BC schools, along with their corresponding meaning.

INTERMEDIATE AND SECONDARY LEVEL GRADE RANGES[4]		
Letter Grade	Percentage Range	Meaning
A	86–100%	Excellent or outstanding achievement
B	73–85%	Very good achievement
C+	67–72%	Good achievement
C	60–66%	Satisfactory achievement
C–	50–59%	Minimally acceptable achievement
F	0–49%	The student has not demonstrated minimally acceptable achievement.
I		In progress or incomplete: The student has not yet done enough to accurately demonstrate learning.
W		Withdrawn from course
SG		Standing Granted: Credit is given, although completion of normal requirements has not been met because of serious illness or another factor out of the student's control.
TS		Transfer Standing: Student is given credit based on learning done in another jurisdiction.
RM		Requirements Met: Given to a student for successful completion of Graduation Transitions (see page 35).

work habits: a student's work ethic and behaviour

Students are also given letters to indicate their **work habits**, such as attendance, attitude, punctuality, and level of respect shown to others. These letters (G for *good*, S for *satisfactory*, N for *needs improvement*) allow the teacher to make a general comment on any number of habits and behaviours that emerge in the classroom.

Additional Evaluation Tools

Your child's learning at the intermediate and secondary levels may be evaluated using one of the following tools.

The Foundation Skills Assessment

The BC Ministry of Education requires students to write the Foundation Skills Assessment (FSA) in Grades 4 and 7. The FSA is a series of six assessments of performance in reading, writing, and numeracy.

The exams are intended to provide an overview of students' learning of foundational skills across the province. In recent years, some controversy has arisen over the FSAs, as some teachers and parents have grown concerned about the amount of time dedicated to preparing for these exams and the perceived stress they place on young students who may not yet be accustomed to exams.

The FSAs include multiple-choice and written components. Students' results are placed into the following categories: performance level unknown, not yet meeting expectations, meeting expectations, or exceeding expectations. Results are mailed to parents or guardians, but do not affect students' final grades.

The FSA takes about four and a half hours to complete, and most schools spread the exams over at least three sessions.

ASSESSMENT AND EVALUATION

PART 5

Note: These graduation requirements are accurate at the time of publication of this book. However, it is important to note that the BC Ministry of Education may change the graduation requirements at any time. Your child should check with the school's counsellor to ensure that his or her courses meet current ministry requirements.

Provincial Examinations

The Graduation Program requires that students write five compulsory provincial examinations:

- a Language Arts 10, Mathematics 10, and Science 10
- a Social Studies 11 or 12
- a Language Arts 12[5]

There are a number of exam sessions scheduled throughout the year to accommodate different program delivery structures.

Students who are not satisfied with their exam scores are able to write any exam a second time without having to retake the course. There is no penalty for retaking a provincial exam; students receive the highest exam mark they achieved, regardless of which attempt resulted in the best score.

PARENT–TEACHER INTERVIEWS

Most schools offer at least one formal opportunity for parents and teachers to meet each year. Parent–teacher interviews may take a variety of forms, including

- individually scheduled parent–teacher interviews held in classrooms or a common space such as a gymnasium
- open houses (drop-in afternoons or evenings) where teachers are available to meet with parents to discuss student progress
- student-led conferences (which students attend with parents) where each student leads a discussion to show both parent and teacher his or her learning and achievement

Student-led conferences give students an opportunity to share their work and accomplishments with their parents. It is a chance for students, parents, and teachers to discuss any issues affecting learning.

Parent–teacher interviews should be seen as opportunities for the caring adults in students' lives to work together to help meet students' learning needs. The following recommendations can help you make the most of these discussions:

- Before the interview, discuss with your child what he or she thinks the teacher might say about his or her work by asking:
  ‣ *What do you think you do well? Why is that?*
  ‣ *What do you think you need to work on?*
  ‣ *What should I ask or discuss with your teacher?*

Prepare for the meeting by asking your child what concerns he or she wants you to discuss.

- During the interview, focus less on your child's grade and more on what he or she is learning, does well, and may need to improve by asking:
  ‣ *What subjects/activities does my child seem to like the most?*
  ‣ *What subjects/activities do you think my child is particularly good at?*
  ‣ *What particular skills does my child need to work on?*
  ‣ *To what extent does my child actively participate in class?*
  ‣ *How does my child get along with other students?*

- Seek clear information about how to encourage and assist your child in his or her learning by asking: *What can I do to help and support my child?*

- Share with the teacher information you think will help him or her understand your child's learning, such as areas where your child has experienced difficulty, any anxiety issues that you have noticed, or other issues that may affect your child's experience. Approach the topic with statements such as:
  ‣ *My child has told me she struggles with... How can I help her with this?*
  ‣ *I have noticed that my child is anxious about... What can we do to help him?*

PART 6

Frequently Asked Questions

KEY QUESTIONS

- How and when will your child's class placement be determined?

- What input can you have in your child's class placement?

- Why do schools have multi-grade classes?

- What makes an effective teacher?

- What happens on professional development days?

- What steps can help to keep your child safe online?

- How can you support your child through school transitions?

- How can you communicate effectively with your child's teacher?

- How can you support your child's learning at home?

- How can you become involved in your child's school?

HOW AND WHEN WILL YOUR CHILD'S CLASS PLACEMENT BE DETERMINED?

School staff try to create the most equitable classes possible. They don't want one class to be significantly larger, or have more students with special needs, than others. Ideally, class placement for the new school year is determined in the preceding spring, based on factors such as

- school population
- class size and composition
- gender balance
- support needs in the classroom, including facility considerations
- teacher preferences
- students' academic abilities, learning styles, work habits, and attitudes
- maturity and age of students
- students' social relationships
- parent requests

Your child may spend the first week of school with the previous year's teacher instead of in a new classroom for any number of reasons, including the following:

- **Staffing allocation from the district is delayed.**
  Schools are usually informed in the spring of their staffing allocation from the school district for the following school year. However, sometimes districts wait until September to allocate staffing numbers, in which case schools have to wait to set up classes until they know how many teachers they will have.
- **Enrollment at the school declines or increases.**
  If the school population changes significantly over the summer, classes set up in the spring may have to be reorganized in September.
- **The school population changes significantly, but the overall number of students stays about the same.**
  In some neighbourhoods, particularly urban inner cities, more than 60 per cent of the population may change from year to year. Classes are set up in September to reflect changes in school population.

WHAT INPUT CAN YOU HAVE IN YOUR CHILD'S CLASS PLACEMENT?

School staff put a great deal of thought into class placement. That said, you are your child's greatest advocate and know your child best. You can request a specific teacher for your child, but it may not always be possible for the school to accommodate your request. Schools generally consider requests that are based on the learning needs of the child, and while social relationships between students can play a role in placement, they are not often a primary factor.

When making a request, match the specific learning needs of your child to the instructional style of the teacher you are requesting. These examples are the types of statements that will give your request credibility:

- My child thrives in environments that are physically active/arts based/_____. I feel that this instructional style is best represented in Ms. _____'s class.
- My child has had conflict with _____ and he/she would be better able to focus on learning if they were in separate classes.
- My child has been coached by Mr. _____ in volleyball and has already created a trusting relationship with him.
- My child's sibling had Ms. _____ in the past and our family has built a strong rapport with her. I would like the opportunity to work with her again.

A positive relationship between students and their teacher helps create an enjoyable and effective learning environment.

WHY DO SCHOOLS HAVE MULTI-GRADE CLASSES?

Multi-grade classrooms (also called *split classes, combined classes,* or *multi-level classes*) date back to the one-room schoolhouses of the 19th century. Financially and logistically, it is almost impossible to run schools without multi-grade classes. Schools tend to be staffed so that primary classes have from 20 to 24 students and intermediate classes have from 25 to 30 students. If a school has 36 Grade 7 students in a school, there are two options:

1. Create two Grade 7 classes of 18 students each, which isn't possible in the majority of schools due to the cost.
2. Create a multi-grade class by dividing the Grade 7 students into two classes and fill the remaining space in one class with Grade 6 students. For example, 25 Grade 7 students are placed in one class, and 9 Grade 7 students are placed in another class with 15 Grade 6 students.

The smaller a school, the more likely it is to have multi-grade classes. Multi-grade classes are also common in schools with an uneven distribution of students between the grades. For example, an elementary school of 600 students could have more than 100 Kindergarten students yet, for demographic reasons, fewer than 50 Grade 4 students.

There are several benefits to multi-grade classes:

- Students learn in different ways and at different rates. Multi-grade classes allow students to learn material above their grade level or review material below their grade level.
- Older students benefit from being role models and leaders. Younger students benefit because they are recipients of peer tutoring.
- Students may form peer and friend groups outside of their grades.

Research shows there are no significant differences in achievement for students in multi-grade classes.[1] Teachers in multi-grade classrooms use a variety of instructional strategies to ensure students are learning the appropriate material. If your child is in a multi-grade class, ask the teacher and principal how the learning needs of your child are being met.

WHAT MAKES AN EFFECTIVE TEACHER?

If you were to interview 30 students who went through the same K–12 school experience and ask them who their favourite teacher was, you would get a huge variety of answers. This is why the notion of an "effective teacher" is not easily defined.

So what *does* make an effective teacher? Much has been written on the topic, but it really comes down to just a few things:

- **Effective teachers are respectful of their learners.**
  They understand the power of words and treat everyone with dignity.
- **Effective teachers are fair and kind.**
  Students don't learn in an environment of fear. Fair and kind teachers have students face consequences for misbehaving or not doing their work, but they are respectful in the process and use the opportunity to teach valuable lessons.
- **Effective teachers connect with their students.**
  They realize that their students are people with emotions, fears, and events in their lives that have an impact on their learning. Effective teachers know what's going on in the lives of their students, and they care.
- **Effective teachers are learners themselves.**
  Advances occur continuously in the field of education. Teachers need to be aware of the research and emerging practices, and strive to put it into action in the classroom.
- **Effective teachers know how best to assess and evaluate their students.**
  Students in an effective teacher's class are aware of what they already know and what they are good at, what they are working on, and how they can improve.

Effective teachers know how best to meet the learning needs of their students, offering support and encouragement when needed.

- **Effective teaching is not about age; it's about skills and ability.**

  Sometimes students and parents think that the young, popular teacher is the one to have as opposed to the older, "old-fashioned" teacher. Some of the most effective and innovative teachers are the experienced ones, who know how to engage and support students as they learn new things. Conversely, sometimes parents believe that older, more experienced teachers are more effective, yet most young teachers are capable, innovative, energetic, and effective educators.

- **Effective teachers understand that each student is different and they adapt their teaching accordingly.**

  The educational term for this is differentiated instruction. Effective teachers know that some students learn best by doing, others by seeing, others by listening, and so on. By differentiating their instruction, teachers find ways for all students to learn and be successful.

differentiated instruction: changing and adapting instructional strategies based on students' needs

- **Effective teachers are effective communicators.**

  Effective teachers communicate with parents by email, by phone, and/or in person. They keep parents informed about their students' learning. Effective teachers also communicate with colleagues, administrators, and counsellors about their students' needs.

- **Effective teachers know, understand, and abide by the rules, regulations, and guidelines of their profession.**

  Teachers in British Columbia are required to follow laws and regulations including the *Manual of School Law*, provincial employment law, collective agreements, and the *Standards for the Education, Competence and the Professional Conduct of Educators in BC.*

Effective teachers use a variety of instructional strategies to keep students engaged and excited about learning.

WHAT HAPPENS ON PROFESSIONAL DEVELOPMENT DAYS?

This is one of the most common questions parents have. Professional development days (often called *pro-D days*) provide opportunities for teachers and other school staff to learn new skills and practices—or to improve upon and enhance existing ones. The collective agreement between teachers and the BC Ministry of Education specifies the number of professional development days that must be held each year in the public system—which, at the time of publication of this book, is six days. Professional development days could focus on topics such as

- implementation of the curriculum and Prescribed Learning Outcomes
- integration of emerging practices and new technologies in the classroom
- assessment and evaluation of student learning
- diverse learner needs, such as students with learning disabilities
- social and emotional well-being and student self-regulation skills

One of the required professional development days is held province-wide. Teachers from all public schools—and many of the independent schools—participate in conferences and workshops, often run by specialist associations such as the BC Association of Mathematics Teachers.

The school administrators often lead one professional development day to focus on the school plan, address student needs, and set goals that must be reported to the Ministry of Education.

> **" Professional development is a process of ongoing growth, through involvement in programs, services, and activities designed to enable teachers, both individually and collectively, to enhance professional practice. "**
>
> —BC Teachers' Federation[2]

At the time of publication of this book, the government has introduced Bill 11: *Education Statutes Amendment Act*, which is expected to pass in the legislative assembly. This Act proposes changes to the *Teachers Act*, including a provision that the Teacher Regulation Branch, upon direction from the Minister of Education, is to set professional development standards such as minimum number of hours and approved content, classifications, or categories of professional development.

FREQUENTLY ASKED QUESTIONS

PART 6

WHAT STEPS CAN HELP KEEP YOUR CHILD SAFE ONLINE?

The Internet can be a powerful learning tool in and outside the classroom, and many teachers find ways to use technology in their teaching. Some teachers find ways to help students communicate with one another and with the teacher beyond school hours, although most schools have guidelines regarding social media use and do not allow teachers to be "virtual friends" with students.

Be vigilant about your child's social media interactions and teach him or her how to be safe online. New social media applications are constantly being developed and the only way to ensure that a child remains safe and secure is for parents to be fully aware of all of their child's online interactions.

Use these tips to help keep your child safe online and help him or her learn how to use social media appropriately:

- Ask your child to tell you about the applications and other online environments he or she uses. Find out what the applications do and how children use them.
- Be aware of how your child is using social media applications and whom he or she is communicating with. Students who abuse social media may set up multiple pages on social media sites with aliases that only their friends know or enter fake birthdates to get access to sites meant for older adolescents.
- Keep the computer in a common area of your home so that you can see what your child is doing online.
- Explain to your child that the Internet is a public space and that the only information that should be posted is information that he or she would be comfortable sharing publicly (for example, to the entire school community).
- Talk to your child about potential consequences of posting inappropriate or disrespectful content.
- Remind your child that, when communicating with strangers, you can't be certain that others are who they say they are. Talk to your child about the dangers of giving out personal information to a stranger.

HOW CAN YOU SUPPORT YOUR CHILD THROUGH SCHOOL TRANSITIONS?

Children are most emotionally and socially vulnerable during times of transition, including when entering Kindergarten and during the changes from primary to intermediate school and intermediate to secondary school, and then from secondary school to the adult world. You can support your child through each of these transitions by providing a stable social and emotional base. Strategies appropriate to each transition stage are outlined in the following sections.

Transition into Primary School

In Kindergarten and throughout their primary education, children learn through play, discovery, collaboration, and socialization. The following strategies may help you support your child during this period of transition:

- Have a positive outlook on what your child is about to experience. Ask what your child is excited about and review all the positive things that have come about as a result of changes in your child's life to date.
- Begin Kindergarten routines a week or two before the start of school. Have your child wake up at the same times and participate in activities similar to ones that he or she will experience in Kindergarten. You may even want to travel to school during the summer weeks so that your child becomes accustomed to the routine.
- Encourage friendships with other students in the class, which can have a huge impact on how children settle into a new environment.

Transition from Primary to Intermediate School

During the transition from primary to intermediate grades, children develop more independence and personal interests. Use the following strategies to support your child during the transition to intermediate school:

- Help your child develop self-confidence. When children feel good about their abilities and their social dynamic, transitions become much easier.

- Talk about the transition with your child as a change that will bring about more choices and opportunities.
- Encourage your child to join clubs, teams, and other extra-curricular activities. The more involved he or she is in the school, the more comfortable the transition will be.
- Ask teachers to help with the transition by describing the opportunities that students may want to pursue when they make the transition into the new grade, class, or school.

Encourage your teen to talk to you about school and his or her social relationships.

Transition from Intermediate to Secondary School

The transition to secondary school coincides with the beginning of adolescence and can be overwhelming for some students. The school environment may be quite different, with students having more than one teacher and moving between classrooms for different subjects. Students may face heavier workloads and be required to show more independence. While in secondary school, students focus on social learning, problem solving, abstract and critical thinking, and information analysis.

Use the following strategies to support your child during the transition to secondary school:

- Remain involved and interested in your child's schooling. Students tend to be more successful when their parents are involved in their education.
- Keep the lines of communication open between you and your teen.
- Understand and keep track of the requirements of the Graduation Program to ensure that your child achieves his or her educational goals.
- Encourage your child to seek support from teachers and guidance counsellors to help cope with the stress of the transition period.

HOW CAN YOU COMMUNICATE EFFECTIVELY WITH YOUR CHILD'S TEACHER?

Effective communication is key to developing a positive relationship with your child's teacher. A good relationship will help you be informed about your child's learning and proactive in resolving any issues that arise. The following strategies can help you build a good relationship:

- Introduce yourself to your child's teacher at the first opportunity. Let him or her know that you are accessible and how best to reach you to discuss any issues affecting your child.

- Keep your child's teacher informed about any issues that may affect your child's learning, such as health concerns or personal circumstances (for example, a divorce or death in the family).

- Ask your child's teacher how you can support your child's learning—both at home and at school. Are there specific learning goals you can work on at home? Does the school need volunteers?

- Attend meet-the-teacher nights, parent–teacher interviews, and any other events that give you the opportunity to discuss your child's learning.

FREQUENTLY ASKED QUESTIONS

PART 6

Communicate with your child's teacher regularly to find out how you can support your child's learning at home.

Questions about assessment methods, disciplinary interventions, and other common issues can be resolved through conversation with your child's teacher.

If you wish to address a specific concern or incident with a teacher, the following strategies can help you maintain a positive and respectful relationship:

- **First, talk to the teacher about your concern.**
  If you go directly to the principal, the principal will likely ask you to meet with your child's teacher.
- **Stay focused on the issue of concern.**
  Let the teacher know how you or your child felt, and express your hopes about how the specific problem can be resolved.
- **Seek clarification and explanations.**
  A child may tell parents part of the truth; he or she may not understand the entire situation. "Can you help me understand…" is a phrase that may help you view the incident from the teacher's perspective.
- **Wait before responding.**
  Instead of writing an emotional email to the teacher as soon as your child gets home, wait until the next day when you can approach the problem rationally and constructively.
- **Sometimes the best outcome is to agree to disagree.**
  You might not always agree with a teacher's decision or the school's handling of a situation, but the incident may have been handled within accepted guidelines.

HOW CAN YOU SUPPORT YOUR CHILD'S LEARNING AT HOME?

Supporting your child's learning at home can reinforce what he or she is learning at school and help develop a lifelong love of learning. The following strategies can help you support your child's learning and overall well-being:

- **Talk to your child about what he or she is learning at school.**
  Ask what topics your child is interested in, what he or she enjoyed that day, and whether there is anything he or she has questions about.
- **Encourage your child to read.**
  When your child is learning to read, read with him or her, and have him or her read to you, encouraging your child to choose which books you read together. Develop a routine, scheduling reading time each day. When your child is older, ask about the books he or she is reading. Read the same books so that you can discuss them together.

Visit the library with your child to help develop a love of books and reading.

- **Help your child establish good work habits.**
  If possible, designate a space in your home and set a regular time each day for homework. Ask your child about his or her assignments, including when the work is due. Encourage your child and help him or her identify work well done.

- **Help your child develop confidence and self-esteem.**
  Help your child express his or her ideas with confidence, learn from mistakes, and undertake new challenges. Help your child set goals—in areas such as academic work, extracurricular activities such as sports or arts, or social and personal responsibility—and support the achievement of those goals.

- **Encourage a healthy lifestyle.**
  Help and encourage your child to develop healthy nutritional habits, participate regularly in physical activity, and get adequate sleep. Limit your child's screen time (that is, time spent watching television, playing video games, or using a computer or other technology).

HOW CAN YOU BECOME INVOLVED IN YOUR CHILD'S SCHOOL?

Research and experience have shown that parental participation in a child's education is a positive contributor to student success.[3] Being involved takes many different forms—not only for each student and his or her family, but also at each stage of the school experience.

In elementary school, especially in the primary years, most children can't wait to include their parents in everything they do and learn, and they welcome their parents at the school or at school events. As students get older, many parents notice their children want them to be less of a presence at the school—and that is a normal, healthy part of growing and learning.

There are many positive ways you can be involved in your child's school and learning, whether it be at the school itself or by nurturing student learning:

- Visit the school and get to know the environment in which your child will be learning.
- Meet the teachers and other staff to put faces to names and allow them to do the same.
- Attend school events such as concerts, sporting events, assemblies, or other special occasions when possible.
- Stay informed about school news and information. Read parent newsletters and sign up for email distribution. Almost all schools have websites (many even use Twitter!)—be sure to check these regularly and then talk with your children about what's happening at school.
- Volunteer when possible. Whether it's at the school or in a way that fits your schedule, it shows your children that what they're doing at school is important.
- Participate in Parent Advisory Council (PAC) meetings. Hearing other parents' perspectives about the school can provide valuable insight. You'll also get to know the parents of your children's classmates and friends.

And perhaps most importantly—ask questions when you don't understand. The bottom line is: everyone is in this together as a team; everyone wants your children to learn, thrive, grow, and succeed.

Many parents extend their involvement from supporting their own child to supporting all children in the school. Through their PACs and DPACs, these parents can create a network of support for all parents and welcome them into the school community.

—BC Confederation of Parent Advisory Councils, 2006[4]

By participating in your school's PAC, you can help make a difference at your child's school.

FREQUENTLY ASKED QUESTIONS

PART 6

Notes

PART 1 How the School System Works

1. Government of British Columbia, *Operating Grants Manual*, 2014/15, 2015/16, 2016/17 (March 2014), http://www.bced.gov.bc.ca/k12funding/funding/14-15/operating-grants-manual.pdf.

2. Ibid.

3. School District No. 41 (Burnaby), *2014/2015 Amended Operating Budget* (February 24, 2015), http://sd41.bc.ca/budgets_policies/AmendBudgetPres2014_2015-1.pdf.

4. BC Ministry of Education, "Classification of Independent Schools," http://www2.gov.bc.ca/gov/content/education-training/administration/legislation-policy/independent-schools/classification-of-independent-schools.

5. BC Ministry of Education, "Grants to Independent Schools," http://www2.gov.bc.ca/gov/content/education-training/administration/legislation-policy/independent-schools/grants-to-independent-schools.

6. BC Ministry of Education, "School Calendar Regulation," http://www2.gov.bc.ca/gov/DownloadAsset?assetId=9612F37D82ED473D81B21C358081BFDF.

7. BC Ministry of Education, *Science Grade 4: From Integrated Resource Package 2005*, http://www.bced.gov.bc.ca/irp/pdfs/sciences/2005scik7_4.pdf.

8. BC Ministry of Education, *English Language Arts 11: Integrated Resource Package 2007*, http://www.bced.gov.bc.ca/irp/pdfs/english_language_arts/2007ela_812_11.pdf.

9. BC Ministry of Education, *Curriculum Development*, https://curriculum.gov.bc.ca/sites/curriculum.gov.bc.ca/files/pdf/curriculum_development_process.pdf.

10. BC Ministry of Education, "BC's Education Plan," http://www.bcedplan.ca/.

11. BC Ministry of Education, "Certificate of Graduation," http://www2.gov.bc.ca/gov/content/education-training/k-12/support/graduation/certificate-of-graduation.

PART 2 Choosing a School

1. Organization for Economic Co-operation and Development (OECD), "PISA 2012 Results," Programme for International Student Assessment (PISA), http://www.oecd.org/pisa/keyfindings/pisa-2012-results.htm.

2. L. W. Lezotte, and K. McKee Snyder, *What Effective Schools Do: Re-Envisioning the Correlates* (Bloomington, IN: Solution Tree Press, 2011).

3. Ibid.

4. School District No. 44 (North Vancouver), "New Registrations—Kindergarten to Grade 12—2015/16 School Year," http://www.sd44.ca/Schools/StudentRegistration/2015_16/Pages/default.aspx.

5. School District No. 23 (Central Okanagan), 405R—*Student Placement (Regulations)*, http://www.sd23.bc.ca/Board/Policies/Section%204%20%20 Students/405R.pdf.

6. BC Ministry of Education—Discover Your School, "Find a School," http://www .discoveryourschool.gov.bc.ca/content/find-school.

   BC Ministry of Education, *Student Statistics*—2014/15 (January 2015), https:// www.bced.gov.bc.ca/reports/pdfs/student_stats/prov.pdf.

7. Khalsa School, "Welcome to Khalsa School!," http://khalsaschool.ca/ uploadedfiles/file/forms/App.pdf.

   Shawnigan Lake School, "Financial Information—Canadian Students," http:// www.shawnigan.ca/ftpimages/589/download/Financial%20Page%20-%20 Cdn.pdf.

8. St. Michaels University School, "Admissions," http://www.smus.ca/ admissions.

PART 3 Program and Schooling Options

1. BC Ministry of Education, *Student Statistics*—2014/15 (January 2015), https:// www.bced.gov.bc.ca/reports/pdfs/student_stats/prov.pdf.

2. A. B. Arai, "Reasons for Home Schooling in Canada," *Canadian Journal of Education* 25, no. 3 (2000): 204–217, http://www.csse-scee.ca/CJE/Articles/ FullText/CJE25-3/CJE25-3-arai.pdf.

3. See note 1 (Part 3).

4. T. Winkelmans, B. Anderson, and M. K. Barbour, "Distributed Learning in British Columbia: A Journey from Correspondence to Online Delivery," *Journal of Open, Flexible and Distance Learning* 14, no. 1 (2010): 6–28.

5. BC Online School, "Course List," http://bc.onlineschool.ca.

6. See note 1 (Part 3).

7. Conseil scolaire francophone de la Colombie-Britannique, "Frequently Asked Questions," http://www.csf.bc.ca/informations/foire-aux-questions/ admission-eng.

8. Ibid.

9. See note 1 (Part 3).

10. BC Ministry of Education, "French Immersion Program," http://www2.gov. bc.ca/gov/content/education-training/administration/legislation-policy/ public-schools/french-immersion-program.

11. Ibid.

12. Alberta Education, "Benefits of Second Language Learning," http://education. alberta.ca/teachers/resources/learnlang/benefits.aspx.

13. École Poirier Elementary School, School District No. 62 (Sooke), *Your Child and French Immersion*, http://www.sd62.bc.ca/Portals/37/Attachments/ French%20Immersion%20brochure%20Poirier.pdf.

14. Edmonds Community School, "Community," http://edmonds.sd41.bc.ca/community.

15. AP Canada, "Participating Schools," http://apcanada.collegeboard.org/participating-schools.

16. International Baccalaureate, "Canada," http://www.ibo.org/en/country/CA/.

17. International Baccalaureate, "Mission," http://www.ibo.org/en/about-the-ib/mission.

18. See note 1 (Part 3).

19. BC Ministry of Education, "First Peoples Principles of Learning," https://www.bced.gov.bc.ca/abed/principles_of_learning.pdf.

20. BC Ministry of Education, "Aboriginal Education Enhancement Agreements," https://www.bced.gov.bc.ca/abed/agreements/brochure.pdf.

21. School District No. 85 (Vancouver Island North), *Aboriginal Education Enhancement Agreement*, http://www.sd85.bc.ca/sd85.bc.ca/new/Teresa%20FN/Enhancement%20Agreement/Enhancement%20Agreement%202_Final.pdf.

22. Nusdeh Yoh, "Aboriginal Choice Program," http://nyohlibrary.weebly.com/about.html.

23. BC Assembly of First Nations, *Governance Toolkit* (2014), Part 1, Section 3.7: Education, http://www.bcafn.ca/documents/GR2S33.7.pdf.

24. Action Schools! BC, "Success Story SD 27 FN Eliza Archie Memorial," http://www.actionschoolsbc.ca/schools-in-action/success-stories/success-story-sd-27-fn-eliza-archie-memorial.

25. School District No. 35 (Langley), "Langley Fine Arts School," http://langleyfinearts.com/about.htm.

26. School District No. 22 (Vernon), "Snowsports," http://www.sd22.bc.ca/Programs/academies/snowsports/Pages/default.aspx.

27. School District No. 43 (Coquitlam), "Elite Performers in Coquitlam Program," http://www.sd43.bc.ca/Programs/Documents/EPIC%20-%20Secondary%20School%20Program%20Information%20Guide.doc.

28. Brentwood College School, "Rowing," http://www.brentwood.bc.ca/athletics/rowing.

29. Western Hockey League, "Prospect Central," http://www.whl.ca/page/prospects-central-current-whl-players.

30. School District No. 38 (Richmond), "About the Montessori Program," http://www.sd38.bc.ca/schools/montessori.

31. Meadowbrook Elementary School, "Principal's Message," https://www.sd43.bc.ca/elementary/meadowbrook/About/PrincipalMessage/Pages/default.aspx.

32. Montessori, "The International Montessori Index," http://www.montessori.edu.

33. School District No. 62 (Sooke), "Gifted," http://www.sd62.bc.ca/Programs/GiftedPace.aspx.

34. School District No. 39 (Vancouver), "MACC: Multi-Age Cluster Class," http://www.vsb.bc.ca/programs/macc-multi-age-cluster-class.

35. BC Ministry of Education, "Secondary School Apprenticeship (SSA)," http:// www2.gov.bc.ca/gov/content/education-training/k-12/support/graduation/ getting-credit-to-graduate/career-and-skills-training/apprenticeship-and -trades/secondary-school-apprenticeship-ssa.

36. College of New Caledonia, "Career Technical Centre," http://www.cnc.bc.ca/ CNC_Programs/Program_websites/Career_Technical_Centre.htm.

37. School District No. 41 (Burnaby), "School to Work," http://sd41.bc.ca/ programs/school_to_work.htm.

38. Vancouver School Board, "Life Skills – Secondary," http://www.vsb.bc.ca/ programs/life-skills-secondary.

39. B. Beairsto, L. Sackney, M. Legacy, and F. Renihan, "Balanced Calendars: The Research and Experience Base," SFU Centre for Educational Leadership and Policy (2013), http://public.sd38.bc.ca/~bbeairsto/Documents/ BalancedCalendarReport.pdf.

     C. Naylor, "Revisiting the Issue of Year-Round Schools," BCTF Research Report (2012), http://www.bctf.ca/uploadedFiles/Public/Publications/ ResearchReports/2012-EI-02.pdf.

40. Imaginative Education Research Group, "The Learning in Depth Program," http://ierg.ca/LID.

41. BC Ministry of Education, "Earning Credit Through Equivalency, Challenge, External Credentials, Post Secondary Credit and Independent Directed Studies," http://www2.gov.bc.ca/gov/content/education-training/ administration/legislation-policy/public-schools/earning-credit-through -equivalency-challenge-external-credentials-post-secondary-credit-and -independent-directed-studies.

42. Ibid.

PART 4 Learning Support and Behaviour Interventions

1.   BC Ministry of Education, "K–12 Funding—Special Needs," http://www2.gov .bc.ca/gov/content/education-training/administration/legislation-policy/ public-schools/k-12-funding-special-needs.

     Government of British Columbia, *Operating Grants Manual*, 2014/15, 2015/16, 2016/17 (March 2014), http://www.bced.gov.bc.ca/k12funding/ funding/14-15/operating-grants-manual.pdf.

2.   BC Ministry of Education, *Special Education Services: A Manual of Policies, Procedures and Guidelines* (September 2013), https://www.bced.gov.bc.ca/ specialed/special_ed_policy_manual.pdf.

3.   Government of British Columbia, *Operating Grants Manual*, 2014/15, 2015/16, 2016/17 (March 2014), http://www.bced.gov.bc.ca/k12funding/ funding/14-15/operating-grants-manual.pdf.

4.   BC Ministry of Education, "Erase Bullying," http://erasebullying.ca/bullying/ bullying-vs.php.

5.   Ibid.

6.   Ibid.

PART 5 Assessment and Evaluation

1. Black, and D. Wiliam, "Inside the Black Box: Raising Standards Through Classroom Assessment," *Kappan Magazine* 92 (2010): 81–90.

    T. J. Crooks, "The Impact of Classroom Evaluation Practices on Students," *Review of Educational Research* 58 (1988): 438–481.

    Western and Northern Canadian Protocol, *Rethinking Classroom Assessment with Purpose in Mind* (2006), http://www.wncp.ca/media/40539/rethink.pdf.

2. Black, and D. Wiliam. (2010). Inside the Black Box: Raising Standards Through Classroom Assessment. *Kappan Magazine* 92: 81–90.

3. BC Ministry of Education, *English Language Arts, Grade 2: Integrated Resource Package* 2006, http://www.bced.gov.bc.ca/irp/pdfs/english_language _arts/2006ela_k7_2.pdf.

4. BC Ministry of Education, *Reporting Student Progress: Policy and Practice* (March 2009), http://www.bced.gov.bc.ca/classroom_assessment/09 _report_student_prog.pdf.

5. BC Ministry of Education, "Certificate of Graduation," http://www2.gov.bc.ca/ gov/content/education-training/administration/legislation-policy/public -schools/k-12-funding-special-needs.

PART 6 Frequently Asked Questions

1. C. Naylor, "BCTF Research Report: Split-Grade and Multi-Age Classes: A Review of the Research and a Consideration of the B.C. Context," BCTF Research Report (January 2000), https://bctf.ca/uploadedfiles/publications/ research_reports/2000ei02.pdf.

2. BC Teachers' Federation, "Professional Development Overview, Policies, and Procedures," http://bctf.ca/ProfessionalDevelopment.aspx?id=6388.

3. S. R. Hara, and D. J. Burke, "Parent Involvement: The Key to Improved Student Achievement," *School Community Journal* 8, no. 2 (1998): 219–228, http://www.adi.org/journal/ss01/chapters/Chapter16-Hara&Burke.pdf.

    W. H. Jeynes, "Parental Involvement and Student Achievement: A Meta-Analysis," *Family Involvement Research Digests*, December 2005, http://www .hfrp.org/publications-resources/browse-our-publications/parental -involvement-and-student-achievement-a-meta-analysis.

4. BC Confederation of Parent Advisory Councils, *Supporting Student Success* (2006), http://bccpac.bc.ca/sites/default/files/supporting_student_success .pdf.

NOTES

CREDITS

NOTES

Glossary

adaptations: alternative teaching and assessment strategies that accommodate the learning needs of a student with special needs

Advanced Placement (AP) program: courses designed to challenge students academically that may earn them credit for a post-secondary course

Annual Instructional Plan (AIP): a learning plan for an English Language Learner

assessment: an ongoing process that helps teachers and students understand how well students are learning; is not graded

balanced-calendar school: a school that operates on a year-round calendar, with classes typically in session for three months, followed by a one-month break

BC Certificate of Graduation (Dogwood Diploma): granted by the BC Ministry of Education upon completion of the Graduation Program

BC Teachers' Federation (BCTF): the union representing all public school teachers in British Columbia

board of education: a board of school trustees that oversees the district's public schools; usually called a school board

catchment area: the area defined by the school district as being served by a particular school

challenge program: a program for elementary students that challenges them beyond the requirements of the regular curriculum

class composition: the number of students with special needs in a classroom

code of conduct: a document that outlines the behavioural expectations for students in a school

collective agreement: a legally binding agreement between an employer and a group of its unionized employees

community school: a school that offers programs when school is out of session and encourages the participation of community residents

Conseil scolaire francophone de la Colombie-Britannique (CSF): the public school district responsible for schools that offer French as the primary language of instruction for students whose first language is French

course credit: a number value assigned to a course as a measure of progress toward completion of a program, such as the BC Certificate of Graduation

curriculum: the content that is prescribed in a course

Daily Physical Activity (DPA) requirements: the minimum amount (30 minutes) of physical activity a student must do during the school day, as specified by the BC Ministry of Education

designation: an identification of a student's special needs, as recognized by the BC Ministry of Education

differentiated instruction: changing and adapting instructional strategies based on students' needs

distributed learning: learning that does not require face-to-face interaction; can be done over the Internet or through direct distribution of course material

District Parent Advisory Council (DPAC): an advisory board at the district level, made up of representatives of PACs from all schools in the district

elective course: a course that is not mandatory but does contribute course credits

evaluation: a judgment on the performance of the student at the end of a unit of study; based on learning outcomes; includes marks/grades

Foundation Skills Assessment (FSA): a standardized test given to BC students in Grades 4 and 7

French immersion program: a program in which French is taught as a second language, but is the primary language of instruction

gifted: a designation given to students with specific, above-average strengths in cognitive areas

Graduation Program: the courses required to obtain the BC Certificate of Graduation (Dogwood Diploma)

Graduation Transitions Program: a required course that includes post-secondary planning, careers research, and healthy living planning

homeschooling: teaching children at home without the supervision of a certified teacher

Individual Education Plan (IEP): a plan based on a student's specific learning needs to help him or her be successful at school

Integrated Resource Package (IRP): curriculum document that includes Prescribed Learning Outcomes, teaching strategies, assessment tools, and resources

International Baccalaureate (IB) program: an academically rigorous program that encourages students to develop global awareness

linear system: a school calendar in which the same courses are taught throughout the year

Ministry of Education: the body designated by the provincial government to oversee K–12 education

modifications: individualized learning goals that reflect a student's educational needs

Montessori: educational philosophy developed by Italian physician and educator Maria Montessori

multi-age cluster class (MACC) program: a program for highly gifted elementary students that provides academic challenge, as well as social-emotional support

multi-grade classroom: a classroom that includes students from more than one grade

outdoor/experiential education program: a school program that emphasizes outdoor learning

Parent Advisory Council (PAC): an advisory board made up of parents of students registered in a school

performance standard: a description of levels of achievement with respect to what students are expected to know and understand

Prescribed Learning Outcomes (PLOs): the specific knowledge, skills, or abilities that students must be able to demonstrate by the end of each course and grade level

professional development day: a day during which teachers focus on developing skills and practices related to teaching; students do not attend school; also called *pro-D day*

Reggio Emilia: educational philosophy developed by Italian educator Loris Malaguzzi

school district: a geographical area, as defined by the *School Act*

semester system: a system used in secondary schools in which the school calendar is divided into two halves called semesters, with students taking half of their yearly courses in each semester of the school year

special needs, student with: a student who has an intellectual, physical, sensory, emotional, or behavioural disability; learning disability; or exceptional gifts or talents

superintendent: the chief administrator of a school district, as designated by the school board

suspension: an intervention in which the student is removed from the classroom for a specified period of time; suspensions may be served at school or at home

Teacher on Call (TOC): a teacher who replaces the permanent teacher during a temporary absence (for example, due to illness); also called a *substitute teacher*

Teacher Regulation Branch (TRB): the body of the Ministry of Education that governs teacher certification and discipline

traditional school: a school that emphasizes traditional instructional models

vocational program: a school program that allows secondary students to specialize in a trade such as carpentry, cooking, or metal fabrication

work habits: a student's work ethic and behaviour

Links

Please be aware that the following links are accurate at the time of publication of this book, but they are subject to change at any time. Pacific Educational Press is not responsible for the contents or reliability of the websites.

PART 1 How the School System Works

GOVERNANCE AND ADMINISTRATION

Ministry of Education

BC Ministry of Education: http://www.gov.bc.ca/bced/

BC Ministry of Education *Manual of School Law* (includes links to the *School Act, Teachers Act, Independent School Act*, and *First Nations Education Act*): http://www2.gov.bc.ca/gov/content/education-training/administration/legislation-policy/manual-of-school-law

BC Ministry of Education—Teacher Regulation Branch: https://www.bcteacherregulation.ca

Board of Education

BC Ministry of Education—Directory of BC K–12 School and District Contact Information: http://www.bced.gov.bc.ca/apps/imcl/imclWeb/Home.do

BC Ministry of Education—Discover Your School: http://www.discoveryourschool.gov.bc.ca

School

BC Teachers' Federation (BCTF): https://www.bctf.ca

Canadian Union of Public Employees British Columbia (CUPE BC)—K–12 Sector: http://www.cupe.bc.ca/cupe-sectors/k-12

BC Principals' and Vice-Principals' Association (BCPVPA): http://www.bcpvpa.bc.ca

BC School Superintendents Association (BCSSA): http://www.bcssa.org

BC Association of School Business Officials (BCASBO): http://www.bcasbo.ca

BC School Trustees Association (BCSTA): http://www.bcsta.org

BC Confederation of Parent Advisory Councils (BCCPAC): http://www.bccpac.bc.ca

FINANCE

BC Ministry of Education—K–12 Funding Allocation System: http://www2.gov
.bc.ca/gov/content/education-training/administration/resource-management/
k-12-funding-and-allocation

Funding for Independent Schools

BC Ministry of Education—Classification of Independent Schools: http://www2
.gov.bc.ca/gov/content/education-training/administration/legislation-policy/
independent-schools/classification-of-independent-schools

BC Ministry of Education—*Independent School Act:* http://www2.gov.bc.ca/gov/
content/education-training/administration/legislation-policy/manual-of
-school-law

HOW GRADE LEVELS ARE ORGANIZED

Elementary Education

BC Ministry of Education. (2000). *The Primary Program: A Framework for Teaching.*
http://www.bced.gov.bc.ca/primary_program/primary_prog.pdf

Secondary Level: Grades 8 to 12

BC Ministry of Education—Graduation: http://www2.gov.bc.ca/gov/content/
education-training/k-12/support/graduation

THE PROVINCIAL CURRICULUM

BC Ministry of Education—Curriculum: http://www2.gov.bc.ca/gov/content/
education-training/k-12/teach/curriculum

BC Ministry of Education—Transforming Curriculum & Assessment (draft
curriculum documents): https://curriculum.gov.bc.ca

BC Ministry of Education—BC's Education Plan: http://www.bcedplan.ca

Graduation Requirements

BC Ministry of Education—Graduation: http://www2.gov.bc.ca/gov/content/
education-training/k-12/support/graduation

PART 2 Choosing a School

WHAT MAKES A GOOD SCHOOL *GOOD*?

Dr. Larry Lezotte's Effective Schools: http://www.effectiveschools.com

HOW TO CHOOSE A PUBLIC SCHOOL

BC Ministry of Education—School Catchment Areas:
http://www.discoveryourschool.gov.bc.ca/content/school-catchment-areas

BC Ministry of Education—Public School Reports (school information and
comparison): http://www.bced.gov.bc.ca/reporting/school.php

BC Ministry of Education—Directory of BC K–12 School and District Contact
Information: http://www2.gov.bc.ca/gov/content/education-training/ways-to
-learn/classroom-learning/public-schools

BC Ministry of Education—Discover Your School:
http://www.discoveryourschool.gov.bc.ca

BC Ministry of Children and Family—For Parents—Looking for Child Care?:
http://www.mcf.gov.bc.ca/childcare/parents.htm

HOW TO CHOOSE AN INDEPENDENT SCHOOL

BC Ministry of Education—Independent Schools:
http://www.bced.gov.bc.ca/independentschools

Federation of Independent School Associations of BC (FISABC):
http://www.fisabc.ca

Independent Schools Association of British Columbia (ISABC):
http://www.isabc.ca

PART 3 Program and Schooling Options

WHAT PROGRAM AND SCHOOLING OPTIONS ARE AVAILABLE?

BC Ministry of Education—Program and Course Options: http://www2.gov.bc.ca/
gov/content/education-training/k-12/learn/program-and-course-options

HOMESCHOOLING

BC Ministry of Education—Homeschooling:
http://www.bced.gov.bc.ca/home_school

BC Ministry of Education—Registering and Protecting Homeschoolers: http://
www2.gov.bc.ca/gov/content/education-training/administration/kindergarten
-to-grade-12/registering-and-protecting-homeschoolers

BC Home Learners' Association: http://www.bchla.bc.ca

Canadian Home-Based Learning Resources: http://www.lifelearning.ca

DISTRIBUTED LEARNING

BC Ministry of Education—Distance Learning: http://www2.gov.bc.ca/gov/content/
education-training/administration/kindergarten-to-grade-12/distance-learning

BC Ministry of Education—Distance Learning Schools: http://www2.gov.bc.ca/gov/
content/education-training/ways-to-learn/classroom-learning/distance
-learning-schools

FRANCOPHONE SCHOOLS

BC Ministry of Education—Language Education Policy: http://www2.gov.bc.ca/
gov/content/education-training/administration/legislation-policy/public
-schools/language-education-policy

Conseil scolaire francophone de la Colombie-Britannique (CSF):
http://www.csf.bc.ca

FRENCH IMMERSION

BC Ministry of Education—French Immersion: http://www2.gov.bc.ca/gov/
    content/education-training/administration/legislation-policy/public-schools/
    french-immersion-program

BC Ministry of Education—French Programs: http://www2.gov.bc.ca/gov/content/
    education-training/ways-to-learn/french-programs

Canadian Parents for French: http://cpf.ca

Canadian Parents for French—BC and Yukon Branch: http://bc-yk.cpf.ca

COMMUNITY SCHOOLS

Association for Community Education in British Columbia (ACEbc):
    http://www.acebc.org

ADVANCED PLACEMENT PROGRAM

BC Ministry of Education—Advanced Placement: http://www2.gov.bc.ca/gov/
    content/education-training/k-12/support/graduation/getting-credit-to-
    graduate/advanced-placement

College Board: https://www.collegeboard.org

AP Canada: https://apcanada.collegeboard.org

INTERNATIONAL BACCALAUREATE PROGRAM

International Baccalaureate: http://www.ibo.org

BC Ministry of Education—International Baccalaureate: http://www2.gov.bc.ca/
    gov/content/education-training/k-12/support/graduation/getting-credit-to
    -graduate/international-baccalaureate

British Columbia Association of IB World Schools: http://www.bcaibws.ca

ABORIGINAL EDUCATION PROGRAMS

BC Ministry of Education—Aboriginal Education: http://www2.gov.bc.ca/gov/
    content/education-training/administration/kindergarten-to-grade-12/
    aboriginal-education

First Nations Schools Association: http://www.fnsa.ca

First Nations Schools Association—School Directory:
    http://www.fnsa.ca/meet-the-schools/list-of-schools

First Nations Education Steering Committee: http://www.fnesc.ca

MONTESSORI AND REGGIO EMILIA PROGRAMS

Montessori Society of Canada: http://www.montessorisocietycanada.org

Montessori Foundation: http://www.montessori.org

North American Reggio Emilia Alliance: http://reggioalliance.org

VOCATIONAL PROGRAMS

BC Ministry of Education—Career and Skills Training: http://www2.gov.bc.ca/
gov/content/education-training/k-12/support/graduation/getting-credit-to-
graduate/career-and-skills-training

Industry Training Authority (ITA): http://www.itabc.ca

Trades Training BC: http://www.tradestrainingbc.ca

OTHER PROGRAMS OF CHOICE

Independent Directed Studies

BC Ministry of Education—Earning Credit Through Equivalency, Challenge,
External Credentials, Post-Secondary Credit and Independent Directed Studies:
http://www2.gov.bc.ca/gov/content/education-training/administration/
legislation-policy/public-schools/earning-credit-through-equivalency-
challenge-external-credentials-post-secondary-credit-and-independent-
directed-studies

PART 4 Learning Support and Behaviour Interventions

WOULD YOUR CHILD BENEFIT FROM ADDITIONAL LEARNING SUPPORT?

What Supports Are Available?

BC Ministry of Education—Students with Special Needs: http://www2.gov.
bc.ca/gov/content/education-training/k-12/support/diverse-student-needs/
students-with-special-needs

BC Ministry of Education—K–12 Funding—Special Needs: http://www2.gov.bc.ca/
gov/content/education-training/administration/legislation-policy/public-
schools/k-12-funding-special-needs

BC Ministry of Education. (2013). *Special Education Services: A Manual of Policies,
Procedures and Guidelines.*
http://www.bced.gov.bc.ca/specialed/special_ed_policy_manual.pdf

How Will Your Child's Needs Be Met in the Classroom?

BC Ministry of Education. (2009). *A Guide to Adaptations and Modifications.*
http://www.bced.gov.bc.ca/specialed/docs/adaptations_and_modifications_
guide.pdf

DOES YOUR CHILD NEED ENGLISH LANGUAGE SUPPORT?

BC Ministry of Education—English Language Learners: http://www2.gov.bc.ca/
gov/content/education-training/k-12/support/diverse-student-needs/english-
language-learners

BC Ministry of Education. (2013). *English Language Learning: Policy and
Guidelines.* http://www.bced.gov.bc.ca/ell//policy/guidelines.pdf

WHAT CAN YOU DO IF YOUR CHILD IS BEING BULLIED?

BC Ministry of Education—ERASE Bullying: http://www.erasebullying.ca

UNDERSTANDING INTERVENTIONS OR SUPPORTS FOR BEHAVIOUR ISSUES

BC Confederation of Parent Advisory Councils. (2006). *Supporting Student Success: Working Together in BC Public Schools.* http://bccpac.bc.ca/sites/default/files/supporting_student_success.pdf

BC Ministry of Education—Student Disputes and Appeals: http://www2.gov.bc.ca/gov/content/education-training/k-12/support/student-disputes-and-appeals

BC Ministry of Education. (1999). *Focus on Suspensions: A Resource for Schools.* https://www.bced.gov.bc.ca/sco/resourcedocs/suspension_resource.pdf

PART 5 Assessment and Evaluation

ASSESSMENT

BC Ministry of Education—Assessment: http://www2.gov.bc.ca/gov/content/education-training/k-12/teach/assessment

BC Ministry of Education—Curriculum and Assessment: http://www2.gov.bc.ca/gov/content/education-training/k-12/support/curriculum-and-assessment

BC Ministry of Education—Transforming Assessment: https://curriculum.gov.bc.ca/assessment

Western and Northern Canadian Protocol. (2006). *Rethinking Classroom Assessment with Purpose in Mind.* http://www.wncp.ca/media/40539/rethink.pdf

EVALUATION

BC Ministry of Education—Student Progress Reports: http://www2.gov.bc.ca/gov/content/education-training/k-12/support/curriculum-and-assessment/student-progress-reports

BC Ministry of Education—Student Reporting Policy: http://www2.gov.bc.ca/gov/content/education-training/administration/legislation-policy/public-schools/student-reporting

Primary Level Report Cards

BC Ministry of Education—Daily Physical Activity: http://www.bced.gov.bc.ca/dpa/dpa_requirement.htm

Intermediate and Secondary Level Report Cards

BC Ministry of Education. (2009). *Reporting Student Progress: Policy and Practice.* http://www.bced.gov.bc.ca/classroom_assessment/09_report_student_prog.pdf

Additional Evaluation Tools

BC Ministry of Education—Foundation Skills Assessment: http://www2.gov.bc.ca/gov/content/education-training/k-12/support/curriculum-and-assessment/foundation-skills-assessment

BC Ministry of Education—Graduation: http://www2.gov.bc.ca/gov/content/education-training/k-12/support/graduation

PARENT–TEACHER INTERVIEWS

BC Teachers' Federation—Parent-Teacher Interviews: http://bctf.ca/parents.aspx?id=3600

The Alberta Teachers' Association—Preparing for Parent-Teacher Interviews: http://www.teachers.ab.ca/Teaching%20in%20Alberta/Resources%20for%20Parents/Parent-Friendly%20Articles/Pages/PreparingforaParentTeacherInterview.aspx

PART 6 Frequently Asked Questions

WHAT HAPPENS ON PROFESSIONAL DEVELOPMENT DAYS?

K. Coates, C. Hodgson, and M. Lombardi. (2009). Everything You Always Wanted to Know About PD Days. *Teacher Newsmagazine (BC Teachers' Federation)* 12(5). https://www.bctf.ca/publications/NewsmagArticle.aspx?id=12792

BC Teachers' Federation—Professional Development and Support: https://www.bctf.ca/ProfessionalDevelopment.aspx

BC Ministry of Education—Training and Professional Development: http://www2.gov.bc.ca/gov/content/education-training/k-12/teach/training-and-professional-development

WHAT STEPS CAN HELP KEEP YOUR CHILD SAFE ONLINE?

BC Ministry of Education—ERASE Bullying: http://www.erasebullying.ca

Canadian Centre for Child Protection—Cybertip!ca: http://www.cybertip.ca

Canadian Red Cross—Kids' Safety Online: http://www.redcross.ca/how-we-help/violence--bullying-and-abuse-prevention/parents/kids--safety-online

Government of Canada—Get Cyber Safe: http://www.getcybersafe.gc.ca/cnt/prtct-yrslf/prtctn-fml/chld-sf-en.aspx

HOW CAN YOU SUPPORT YOUR CHILD THROUGH SCHOOL TRANSITIONS?

BC Ministry of Education—Back-to-School Tips: http://www2.gov.bc.ca/gov/content/education-training/k-12/support/back-to-school-tips

Government of Alberta—Common Questions—How can my child prepare for the transition from...: http://www.learnalberta.ca/content/mychildslearning/commonquestions.html

HOW CAN YOU BECOME INVOLVED IN YOUR CHILD'S SCHOOL?

BC Confederation of Parent Advisory Councils. (2006). *Supporting Student Success: Working Together in BC Public Schools.* http://bccpac.bc.ca/sites/default/files/supporting_student_success.pdf

BC Confederation of Parent Advisory Councils (BCCPAC): http://www.bccpac.bc.ca

LINKS